Stories From The Other Side…

Conversations With Those Who Passed Away

Second Edition

"There are more things in Heaven and Earth, Horatio, than are dreamt of in your philosophy"

— William Shakespeare
Hamlet

Stories From The Other Side
Conversations With Those Who Passed Away
Anny Slegten

Published by
Kimberlite Publishing House
www.kimberlitePublishingHouse.com

©2018 by Anny Slegten   20241215

All Rights Reserved. Manufactured by Amazon.ca

No part of this book may be reproduced, stored in or introduced into a retrieval system, or transmitted, in any form or by any means – electronic, mechanical, photocopying, recording or otherwise – without the prior written permission of the copyright owner.

The author of this book does not dispense medical advice or prescribe the use of any technique as a form of treatment for physical, emotional, mental, spiritual, or medical problems without the advice of a physician, either directly or indirectly. The intent of the author is only to offer information of a general nature to help you in your quest for physical, mental, emotional, and spiritual wellbeing. In the event you use any of the information in this book for yourself, which is your right, the author and the publisher assume no responsibility for your actions.

ISBN: 978-1-7752489-1-0
Book layout by Colin Christopher *www.colinchristopher.com*
Book cover and Kimberlite Logo designed by
Marietta Miller *www.execugraphx.com*

The Kimberlite Diamond Connection

Kimberlite is a rock type that was first categorized over a 100 years ago based on descriptions of the diamond-bearing pipes of Kimberley, South Africa.

Kimberlites are the mechanism by which diamonds are brought to the surface.

Kimberlitic rocks are the most important primary source of diamonds and the main rock type in which significant diamond deposits have been found so far.

Anny is familiar with many rocks and minerals as her husband was raised around quarries, and later worked in several mines in Canada.

Therefore, it was natural for Anny to choose kimberlite as an analogy to the soul residing within our body – as a diamond within the kimberlite.

Dedication

Dear Frank, Helen, Kari, Kelly, Marilyn, Peter, Terry, Theresa and Toni:

As promised, I dedicate *Conversations With Those Who Passed Away* to you, the Hypnotism Training Institute of Alberta classes of spring and summer 2002. It was quite an upbeat class; we laughed at ourselves, and the learning was great.

"Do you have something written about this?" was the question after each hypnosis and hypnotherapy technique explanation and demonstration. I did not. The reason for the question was obvious. I knew you were right and as usual; let you nag me about it.

This started a lot of writing, and enjoying it too, the reason I promised you to dedicate this book to you!

You were the major influence at getting me to write information down – and I thank you for it.

You know I love you all.

Anny

Acknowledgements

Those to whom I express my gratitude would fill several books: my parents, teachers, instructors, colleagues, friends, clients, students and graduates in both hypnotherapy and Reiki who are now my peers, most of you living on this plane, and some having crossed over to the other dimension.

In hypnosis as well as in Energy private one-on-one sessions and during training classes, you trusted me with your deepest thoughts, sharing your joys, your dreams, your struggles and miseries.

Life is a journey and I learned to listen with my heart, asking you to help me help you, and you did. Although most of us planned our journey as a challenge, you all taught me to look at myself and discover the incredible privilege of being a human being, a spirit having decided to have a physical experience on planet Earth.

While I was born in Belgium, this journey of mine started in Léopoldville, now known as Kinshasa, in what used to be Belgian Congo.

I was eighteen months old. I am so glad my parents took me along with them. Although we had to leave twenty-three years later, losing what I believed was my forever country, I still consider it a blessing and a privilege to have been raised there, attending the Lycée du Sacré Cœur de Kalina, a Catholic school run by Les Dames du Sacré Cœur (The Ladies of the Sacred Heart).

These Catholic nuns/teachers were exceptional in their wisdom and their awareness about what life is all about, and they started my quest about "there is more."

To each and every one of you, thank you!

Anny

An Important Message

With the exception of two case histories that happened spontaneously, the contents of *Conversations With Those Who Passed Away* are transcripts from recorded or filmed private hypnotherapy sessions or surrogate hypnotherapy sessions.

When doing a surrogate session, it is important to voice everything that is coming to our awareness as is – without judgment and without paraphrasing. This is done to absorb the content as it is presented by the spirit of the subject connected – as they intend it to be.

When experiencing the mind-to-mind connection, the communication is at two levels of understanding, resulting in the phrasing often being different from the way we talk.

As you are reading *Conversations With Those Who Passed Away*, please bear in mind this very important point:

What you see in print is exactly as it was presented to maintain the authenticity of the session. Therefore, please read to understand the concepts from different cultures and mother tongues since each have their own unique ways of expressing themselves. And this is respectfully maintained.

Foreword

by Colin Christopher

Anny Slegten offers unconventional observations of life and death that are sure to raise questions about your own personal perceptions and beliefs.

When it comes to helping people, Anny is a world-class clinical hypnotherapist with a lifetime of experience. She has taught hypnotherapy longer than most hypnotherapists have been in private practice and is on the leading edge of hypnotherapy technique development.

This book contains a selection of the very best of Anny's *thousands* of recorded hypnotherapy sessions, to illuminate a provocative and often-thought-about topic: *What happens to you after you die?*

When it comes down to it, the reason you decide to seek help with hypnotherapy is to better yourself in some way. When the desire to better yourself occurs— whether by breaking a bad habit, becoming more successful, dealing with relationship issues, or grieving and loss, among others—you will decide to seek help when you are ready to have a good look at yourself and make some improvement.

In private sessions, hypnotherapists help clients improve their lives by facilitating the pursuit and achievement of *peace of mind*. This is done in a way that nurtures and fosters healing, transformation and growth in the client seeking personal betterment.

When pursing peace of mind in the hypnotherapy chair, themes of life and death often emerge—for a variety of reasons. To be effective and help their clients, hypnotherapists must approach, facilitate and aid in the resolution of these themes of life and death.

Conversations With Those Who Passed Away paints a picture of birth, life, death and the afterlife with case studies from the hypnotherapist's viewpoint, to show you a way of thinking very different from the conventional knowledge you may be familiar with.

When picking up this book, ask yourself, "Am I seeking peace of mind?"

If you answer yes, this book will help you do so.

As a successful author and professional speaker, I recognize and understand the profound value of having the right person help me achieve peace of mind. When it comes to hypnotherapy, Anny Slegten is the professional I call on when I am looking for ways to effect improvement within myself. Her wisdom and experience in hypnotherapy is unequalled, and I take full advantage of it to better myself.

Better yourself by taking advantage of Anny's knowledge and read *Conversations With Those Who Passed Away* to see life from a refreshing, unique and stirring perspective.

Colin Christopher
Author, *Success through Manipulation*
Chicago, Illinois
February 25, 2013

Introduction

Our other side of the self has been fascinating me for a long time. In an old black-and-white film I have watched twice in a span of no less than 30 years, I observed an experiment in laboratory where, at a man's exact time of death, there was a loss of three grams (one-tenth of an ounce). No loss was registered when an animal died. I also observed tests in laboratory showing that a plant confined in a room reacted when the same type of plant located in another room was cut down.

This was fascinating information to me. What is about Energy that makes a body lose three grams at time of death? Since then, I have learned that some people at the bedside of a dying person see the soul leave the body. Yes, we have a condensed Energy within us. It is like the light of the Divine, whoever or whatever one perceives the Divine to be. To my understanding, it is located in a little cavity at the tip of the heart. I call it our celestial battery.

Being raised Catholic, of course I knew about what are called purgatory, heaven, and hell. Because of many stories, I knew also about earthbound entities we call ghosts. However, it is when I started to practice hypnosis and hypnotherapy that two and two makes four.

We are Energy people who decided to have a physical experience. How we judge ourselves once we discard our physical body reveals the reason we perpetuate the cycle of death, birth, physical life, death, birth, physical life, death ... and here we go again.

Some cultures believe the body is just a shell around the real self. Once dead, the shell is simply buried—no fuss, no mark, no tombstone, nothing. In other cultures, the physical death is regarded as waking up from a dream and entering the real life, the life of the soul. From what some people go through in life, it looks more like waking up from a nightmare to me. Somehow, deep down, we know there is something more after death with no certainty of what comes next

In my full-time practice as a clinical hypnotherapist since 1984, my clients have taught me what happens when what is commonly known as a ghost decides to attach itself to a person. Who these ghosts are, where they live and what they are inclined to do can be surprising.

My clients made me discover that the *other part, that Energy part,* of ourselves is *two years ahead* of our physical experience. This awareness helps me understand the death of a person by asking what happened *two years* prior to the person's death, or *two years* before an illness started. To my understanding, it is usually experiencing something heart breaking instilling a fear of the future. The result is an unconscious inner feeling of dying.

The first time I became aware of this was in the beginning of my private hypnotherapy practice when a client came to me explaining that he felt the urge to get into his car and kill himself in a single-car accident. The session revealed that his mother had died *two years* prior to my client coming to see me. Since his mother's death, my client's actions had made him lose everything — work, career, investment, home and family. He had burned all his bridges, ready to die. What did that have to do with his mother? His mother had been very sick throughout her pregnancy, and my client, while still in his mother's womb, had decided, "if mother dies, I die."

Yes, there is a parallel universe. Mr. Hugh Everett III, a scientist who studied quantum physics, was the first to announce that a parallel universe exists. You can read the various accounts of that on the Internet.

To discover who we really are as human beings is a fascinating journey. In spite of all that has been presented to me, I realize that there is still more to learn.

Anny

Disclaimer

The intent of the author is to share information of a general nature to help the reader in search of personal understanding and education.

In the event of physical, emotional, mental and spiritual discomfort, it is the reader's responsibility to consult with appropriate professionals.

The applications of perceived methods, protocols and information given in *Conversations With Those Who Passed Away* are the choice of each reader, who assumes full responsibility for his or her actions.

The author and the publisher of this book assume no responsibility for the reader's understandings, interpretations, actions, choices or results.

Please note, *the names, gender or places may be changed to protect the privacy of everyone concerned.*

Table Of Contents

The Kimberlite Diamond Connection 5
Dedication 7
Acknowledgements 9
An Important Message 11
Foreword 13
Introduction 17
Disclaimer 21
Table Of Contents 22
Chapter - 1 - 27
   Any Questions? 27
Chapter - 2 - 37
   The Discovery 37
      The story of Nita 42
      What happens when we die? Who are these ghosts?. 47
Chapter - 3 - 53
   What Signals Earthbound Entities? 53
      By making you know they are there with you 53
      By appearing to you 54
      By a client during a regular hypnotherapy session 55
      By a surrogate hypnotherapy session 55
      By "playing" with the Ouija board 63
      For some people, a physical sensation 66

Chapter - 4 - 69

What Happens Once The Physical Body Is Dead? 69
The many reasons to stay earthbound. 69
John the Banker: Not wanting to leave. 70
Anybody there? 73
The story of Sally: Not knowing her body was dead .. 74
The Lumber Jack: Not knowing where to go. 77
The story of Jodi: The grieving kept her earthbound 79
A mother's unfinished business 87
The possessive wife 88
A ghost at the rescue of a dying baby 91
The story of Jonathan's uncle 93
The young girl and the knife 95
What are the signs of the presence of a ghost? 97
The lady whose father had passed away: TV changing channels 97
Waiting and wishing they arrive: Feeling uncomfortable 98
The Story of Marianne: Getting sexually aroused for no apparent reason 99

Chapter - 5 - 111

Ghosts In Houses, Buildings And Land 111
A cultural belief 111
The new restaurant on the lake shore 112
Schaeffer the gambler 124

Chapter - 6 - 141

Home At Last 141
The story of Bernard 143
The road to what we call eternity, heaven 154

Afterword 159
Hypnotherapy, A Healing Modality 161
Online Store, Contact, And More… 166
Other Books By Anny 167
Glossary / Description 168
About Anny - The Author 175

CHAPTER 1

Chapter - 1 -

Any Questions?

Writing *Conversations With Those Who Passed Away* generated many questions, first among them, what is the point of this book, and what message do I want to convey?

What I really want from writing and publishing *Conversation With Those Who Passed Away*, as well as the many other books still in their infancy, is the same thing as when people come to see me for private hypnotherapy sessions: to help people achieve comfort and peace of mind, whatever that may mean to them. Being at peace with oneself is truly the key to mental health, sound decisions, a pleasant life and peaceful death. How you will achieve this by reading *Conversations With Those Who Passed Away* is up to you. I am presenting you with a candle, and you alone can light your way.

For whatever reason, many cultures regard death as a defeat, losing the battle of life. Listening to what most people say when talking about death, it is no wonder death is looked upon as the final stage of life. In fact, it is simply a transition from life with its encumbrance of all the physical challenges we had planned to experience, back to our place in the Energy Field. Yes, there is an afterlife, and once there, our conscience makes us reflect on all we have done.

Connecting with the spirits of dead beings has brought the experience of physical death into light. There are two stages to go through once the spirit has discarded the physical body. The first stage is staying earthbound, close to home. As it disconnects from the body, the spirit evaluates the life it just left, and whatever is on its mind then will make it come back to another physical experience. As they move from a physical experience to a non-physical experience, the Energy will take the form of what the spirit expects to see or encounter, until the earthbound entities come to their senses.

As explained in the movie The Tibetan Book of the Dead available at the National Film Board of Canada, at the time of death "... *we project our own emotional state and then we believe it is the real world*".

Earthbound entities (most commonly referred to as *ghosts*) taught me in our encounters that the best way to get their cooperation is to regard them and treat them as I would have in their physical body. That includes respect and, most of all, making them talk about themselves and letting them explain the reason they did not move on to the next plane. When earthbound, the spirits are mostly preoccupied with the life and activities they just left and are sometimes scared to move forward to what they perceive as the unknown, stretching their comfort zone.

There is a good reason this place is also called Purgatory. Once on the other side of the veil, it is the only time a soul may "purge" their mistakes, make amendments, and even repair their errors –usually made in total ignorance.

Staying there to do the work takes courage, and finding themselves untangled from their own ego cleanses the soul – setting them free and clearing the way to a much better sojourn in what is called heaven and their next physical life.

The soul is then free to decide to stay to help a loved one they left behind, or to move to the next level, and this for many reasons.

Some souls want to go straight to what is called heaven – not having the courage to look at themselves. The result is pure hell as they are stuck in their self-judgment.

The second stage is returning to the pure Energy Field, a place most commonly known as eternity or heaven.

The experience of moving into the Universal Energy is always the same, regardless of religion or lack of it. Reuniting with one's pure essence, moving into the Energy Field can be compared to swimming underwater and then breaking through the surface for a breath of fresh air.

It is a portal perceived as a soft bright light. From what I was made to understand, breaking through is a most exhilarating experience, and once there it becomes an individual experience. Then comes reflection of what happened during the life just left; often spirits realize they were on a treadmill, doing the same thing over and over again.

That time of reflection then becomes unbearable. One could call it pure hell, as the soul experiences regrets for what happened or did not happen, from seeking forgiveness to seeking revenge, and anything in between.

Being of pure essence, pure energy, has nothing to do with being holy. *Pure* in this context means maximum potency, not holiness or sainthood.

As inconceivable as it is, it is at that time that you make a detailed plan of what you want to experience next, wanting to release what sits so heavily on your conscience, your soul. Whatever your reason, you are a spirit wanting to have a physical experience. What you are planning to release is the result of your thoughts as you physically died. Yes, your thoughts count, especially at the time of death. Hell and heaven are not places, but states of being. And you are the one who creates them. You are the cruelest when judging yourself.

Compare your soul to a diamond in the rough. Without realizing it, and not paying attention to the details and how you want to experience it, you then choose to experience a life abrasive to you, to polish your soul into what you perceive as a most beautiful diamond. Think about it: what is the difference between wanting to experience forgiveness and wanting to have the pleasure of experiencing forgiveness? Wanting to have children and wanting to have the pleasure of having children?

I did my best to include case studies about all this, editing only personal information to keep the confidentiality of my clients and students intact. Parts of the transcripts have been summarized to remove repeated comments.

Listening to what the spirits of the ones who passed away had to share was an enlightening experience, the reason I am publishing *Conversations With Those Who Passed Away*. Choosing from thousands of recorded or filmed sessions was not an easy task. I did my best to choose the experiences to enlighten you as well.

When do I see and converse with spirits? Am I psychic? Did I always possess the psychic abilities I have now? It all depends on how one perceives what it is to be a psychic. Personally, I do not think I am psychic. When choosing to do so, I see, feel, hear and smell what goes on when in a hypnotic trance facilitating one-on-one hypnotherapy sessions.

The clearest connection I experience is when I am a surrogate in a deep hypnotic trance during what we call *remote* or *surrogate* sessions, a virtual healing modality I developed decades ago. In fact, it is giving the client who requested the session for an investigation and/or healing session of what is going on with themselves or with someone else.

The information regarding the person, dead or alive, land or place comes from a nonphysical source. In that modality, the origin of everything reveals itself: Past lives, in the womb, this life, spirit attachments, as well as curses and spells.

Bypassing the brain, the mind-to-mind connection is then crystal clear to me, being with a person alive or a person who passed away. To my understanding, the requirement is to trust whatever awareness comes to mind. I learned to trust my intuition, the tuition that comes from within, no questions asked. My intuition, that awareness that comes to me as a strong psychic voice, serves me well and has for as long as I can remember.

As my graduate hypnotherapist students often explain, trusting the way the information comes to mind, no matter what, trusting the first thing that comes to mind and staying grounded, is something I keep reinforcing from day one during the complete hypnosis and hypnotherapy training. The obvious reward comes during Hypnosis and the Paranormal, one of the most advanced hypnotherapy courses I teach, when students learn to successfully connect mind-to-mind with the subject to perform a surrogate hypnotherapy session.

As you are reading *Conversations With Those Who Passed Away* please forgive my phrasing, which is not always easy to follow. English is the fifth language I learned to speak, and my choice of words is directly connected to the ease of pronunciation. This book is in English, because the training I took, and still take to polish my diamond, was and is English.

It is important for my writing to resemble the way I talk. I want you to realize I am truly the one who wrote the book, though I know the way I express myself is rather funny at times. Having experienced life on three continents and the cultures of Europe, Central Africa and North America, I developed a unique way of explaining the inexplicable.

Although not always in agreement with me, my editor did an excellent job of keeping a comfortable balance between maintaining my voice and making my message clear and easy for you to understand. I am grateful that she skillfully polished the way I express myself in proper English, keeping intact my personal writing style.

====================================

CHAPTER 2

====================================

Chapter - 2 -

The Discovery

Is there another side to life? What experience do you believe you will encounter as you die?

I have heard some people wonder if there will be a black hole, while others envision people carried away on a gold chariot, and still others believe they will float on a cloud wearing a nice, flowing, long white gown, with wings and playing the harp—and everything in between. From what the entities taught me, whatever they believe or experience will be there, until they come to their senses.

There are many signs indicating something is going on, especially when things go bump in the dark. There is nobody there, although there is somebody there: footsteps, squeaky floors, slamming doors, slamming toilet seats, the scent of a pipe, voices.

Cats—who can see entities clearly—look at something, although according to you there is nobody there; dogs bark at what you think is nothing, their hair standing up on their backs.

TVs change channels on their own, appliances and battery-powered gadgets start on their own, the telephone rings once with an unfamiliar sound, and, as one of my clients experienced, her cell phone acted up in a funny way. Not so funny is when, seeking vengeance, an earthbound entity disrupts the complete electrical system of a building, as well as all its automatic or remote electrical functions.

There is a world alive and well on the other side of our physical world. We know about ghosts, sometimes scary and sometimes intriguing, as they make us aware of their presence in homes, buildings and open spaces. I was not aware of a ghost attaching itself to a human being until four ghosts who had attached to one of my clients made themselves known during a hypnotherapy session. It was obvious that my client's issues originated from these four attachments.

As I started to do an exorcism ritual on them, they became violent. I feared for the recliner my client was sitting in, as each one of them, in turn, would pound on it, expressing themselves through my client. I was sure that at this rate, my recliner would be in pieces.

Addressing my client (referred to as the *host*) by her first name, I said, "*One, two, three, open your eyes.*" At that command, my client opened her eyes, and I explained to the entities that I knew they were present and that I would get them to leave in another way.

The other way was by surrogate session, a hypnotherapy session at a distance, the technique I had developed a many years, or is it many lives before. The surrogate hypnotherapy session, which we often call a remote session, was violent too, although easier to perform than when working directly with the host.

Looking back at what I have learned since about the lives of the spirits living where ghosts are roaming, I realize now that these ghosts were very frightened and responded appropriately to the way I was going about releasing them. Understanding these spirits, learning who these entities were, floating between two worlds, and why they were around led to knowing how to get their cooperation, to go home through the Light willingly and get on with their lives. It reminds us too that there is a world out there alive and well that we do not see with our physical eyes.

There are different levels of possessions. Possession can be complete, taking over a person's body and life. This type of possession, sometimes referred to as multiple personality disorder or dissociative identity disorder, affects the person's behavior, memory, career choices and state of health.

Other times, entering the person's aura, In this instance, the entity nags and bugs their prey until the person gives up and complies to shut off the nagging ... until it starts all over again.

Staying near the person and outside a person's Energy field. This happens when a person has strong boundaries. The symptoms are minor.

Energy is everything and everything is Energy. Yes, with a capital E.

The Energy of our spirit is the essence, the life force of who we are, and carries our disposition and our memories. The entities we connect with have no qualms about expressing their views and feelings.

Although sometimes dramatic, encounters with spirits can be very funny. For me, the best way to understand these nonphysical guests is to establish rapport. This also makes it much easier to send them home.

When working with them to establish rapport, I usually ask their name, and how they like to be addressed. Without hesitation, one once answered, ""F— you."

Without blinking an eye, I answered, "Hello, F— You," and proceeded with the session to find a way to make him decide to go through the Light and get on with his life.

Five minutes into the connection, *F— You* started to laugh and said, "My name is Richard."

Who are these entities? Where are they coming from?

They are in fact the souls of dead persons who find themselves stuck, earthbound. Having shed their physical bodies, these disincarnate entities are in limbo, in purgatory, in a grey area, and many times lost, having no idea of where to go. One could call that state living *where ghosts are roaming*. Earthbound entities are living persons without a body and carry with them their dispositions, fears, phobias, likes and dislikes. They can be very mischievous too, just as when having a physical body. At that stage of existing, having no life, the souls are far from holy.

They should have gone through the portal on the way to their Energy pod, their home in the universe. We all come from there. Our soul is concentrated Energy and part of the Universal Energy. We are pure Energy, and our individuality makes it concentrated, resulting in being an individual, a pod, within the whole, the Universal Energy.

When I wish to psychically see them during a one-on-one hypnotherapy session, I simply ask the entities I am working with to do something to enable me to see them. History comes alive. The most impressive entity was one of a very wealthy man from Mongolia.

He had been attached to my client, a son he had lost in a train crash so long ago. He was impressive, riding a white horse. He had a kind of goatee, and his clothes were made of absolutely beautiful silk. I complimented him about them.

The story of Nita

As a client accessed a life prior to this one while in a hypnotic trance, an entity made herself known by starting to scream: *"I do not want to die! I do not want to die!"* at the top of her lungs.

As my client looked at me, terrified, I immediately realized this was not her at all, that there was someone else there.

Calming her down, I asked her: *"What is your name? How do you like to be addressed?"*

Surprised, and looking at me, she said, *"Nita."*

Anny: "Hello, Nita! ... You look surprised I am calling you by name. It has been a long time since someone talked to you directly, is it not?"

And eyes wide open, in total delight, she said slowly: "*Yes!*"

Her glassy eyes looked very different from Lucia's, the host's, and I knew Nita was in fact what is called an "alter." This was total possession.

I could psychically see her. She was a very pretty young girl, naked. I could tell she was from Africa. She had beautiful legs, medium-dark brown skin and smooth, long, black hair. She was very upset at having been strangled to death.

Anny: "*And?*"

Still very upset, with great gestures, she explained she had been thrown on a pile of garbage.

Gesturing, I replied: *"So?"* refraining from adding, *"Who cares? You are still here!"*

Surprised, she kept silent about a minute, reflecting on my matter-of-fact approach.
As the conversation went on, I asked Nita if she knew how beautiful she was.

She proudly explained that she was very pretty and was sold at a very high price because of it. As the strong telepathic connection unfolded, it was obvious she knew she was very valuable, by the price her owner had paid to acquire her as a slave. She had a sense of superiority and felt she could just do as she pleased, doing absolutely nothing, and had the attitude and temper of a very spoiled girl. At one point, I asked her, *"Look back at your life: what have you learned?"*

The answer was straight and to the point: *"Being pretty is not enough. You have to work too."*

In a deep trance myself, and trusting my intuition to make Nita leave Lucia the host, and go through the Light on her own accord, I explained to her that once having gone through the Light, she could come back as a gorgeous lady and become an internationally acclaimed fashion model, travelling all over the world.

Looking at me, full of anticipation, she said: *"Could it be?"*

I assured her that if she wanted it, it would be so. And she agreed to leave.

This was a total possession, and Nita's host was "not there," totally unaware of what had gone on. Interestingly enough, after the session, when I explained what had unfolded, Lucia exclaimed, *"That is where it came from!"*

Although not at all interested in being a fashion model, Lucia had taken modelling training and at one point was a fashion model because she felt she had to do it.

In a case of total possession, the alter takes over, and the host is completely out of the physical body, with no recollection of what is happening, only to *come to*, wondering what happened. Sharing the conversation I had had with Nita, I knew by Lucia's facial expression that I was explaining many things Lucia had experienced while wondering what happened: this was not her!

Now Lucia understood what happened one time when she visited her parents and had an argument with her mother. Nita must have been triggered and presented herself in Lucia, who became hysterical and started to scream at her mother. She jumped up and down and later did not really remember what she said. The disbelieving way Lucia's mother looked at her made her come to as she stopped and thought, *Why the heck did I just do that?*

Lucia's mother looked at her as if she did not know her, and Lucia felt as if she were not there. Upon reflection, when she left her parents' house, she was quite scared, because she knew that it was not she who had just done that.

Saying nothing to Lucia, I simply kept in touch to know what happened since Nita went through the Light, setting Lucia free. Lucia's interests shifted in a very dramatic way, and with much relief I observed that she was still married.

In a total possession, the alter is in full control of what goes on with the host. I was wondering if Lucia was in agreement with Nita about the choice of husband she had married. In other words, whose husband was that man. Nita's, Lucia's, or both? Had the alter been male, Lucia would most likely have been attracted to a woman of the male alder's choice and thus would have entered into a lesbian relationship.

How can this be?

Compare your body to a car and your soul to the driver of that car. Not wanting to be present or experience a situation can be compared to stopping the car you are driving and getting out of it, door open, engine running.

Talk about an opportunity for a bored, disincarnate entity who longed to drive to get into that car, engine running, and drive it until having enough of it or even until another disincarnate entity wanted its turn at the wheel and later returned the car to the owner, who has no idea of what happened while entities were at the wheel, totally *out of it* while someone else was driving the car.

This is the simplest way I can explain a full possession. When coming to, returning to awareness, the possessed person has no idea of what made them do what they did.

One also wonders whose events keep coming to a person's awareness: theirs or someone else's?

As I explained earlier, there are many levels of psychic interference, from total possession, taking over the person's life, affecting their career, their memories, their hobbies, and their health, to sticking their nose in that person's affairs.

Some ghosts have good intentions, some ghosts are mischievous, some are miserable, some are good-natured, the way they were when in their physical form. Their reason, their *what for*, to attach to human beings varies, depending on their disposition, their last thoughts and what happened as they died. Knowing ghosts made me realize our incarnate being is the reflection of who we really are on the non-physical side of life. We stay the same until we wake up to inner peace.

What happens when we die? Who are these ghosts?

I have learned to let the essence of the spirits talk about their experiences, their thoughts and their feelings at time of death and beyond.

What became obvious is that our conscience lodges in our mind, the nonphysical part of us, the reason we can access past lives. As incredible as it is, it is at the moment of death, as we are reviewing our life in a twinkling of an eye, that we plant the seed that will make us come back to atone for the emotion that sits heavily on our conscience. Everything about us stays with us.

Wilder Penfield, one of the greatest neuroscientists who ever lived, admitted that the "I," as he called the soul, and the brain are not the same thing. The mind is nonphysical and aloof from the brain.

This reminds me of a client in her mid-twenties. I do not remember the reason this client came. However, I remember the session clearly. While making herself comfortable in my recliner, my client explained that since she had taken street drugs, her physician had explained, her memory was damaged by holes in her brain. Smiling, I explained to her that since the memory is in the mind, the nonphysical part of us we access when in a hypnotic trance, having holes in her brain had nothing to do with her memory. And my client, who was very responsive when entering a hypnotic trance, had very clear recollections of events since her preteens and remembered them clearly once out of the trance.

Every spirit I connected with made me understand there are two stages after death. The first one is experiencing life without the encumbrance of a physical body. This is limbo, in the grey area also known as purgatory. When connecting with these entities during a surrogate hypnotherapy session, I psychically see them as though they were still in their physical body, and their concerns are normal everyday concerns with work and play, visiting places and families and, usually, attending their own funeral.

Once they have gone through the Light, they show themselves without a face, only the outlines. At this stage, reflecting on what is sitting heavily on their conscience, they are deciding what to do next to shake off whatever is sitting so heavily on them. It is then that they establish a detailed plan on how to atone. Yes, we all make our own plan of action at that time.

To understand our essence as human beings, again compare the body to a car and the soul as the driver of that car. Notice that the maker of the car tempts us to buy it by advertising and so forth. However, it is the buyer who is the owner of that car, and usually the driver too.

A woman, your future mother, is in the cycle of offering a body to a soul. It is your soul who decides to take the opportunity to have a physical experience, incorporating your Energy, your life force, to create the process of conception and reincarnation. Understanding that your reason to come back is always to put closure to unfinished business, the last thought as you died, you realise you chose your mother, the family, the ethnic background, the gender, the culture, the religion, the country, the living conditions for your good—nobody else's! As we reincarnate, we are in a sense taking on a package deal.

So, what make us susceptible to having an entity attach to us, and what makes an entity want to stay earthbound? The reasons are as varied as our personalities. The only way to know is to connect with the essence of a person, dead or alive. For Lucia, it was vacating her body to avoid an unpleasant experience, giving Nita the opportunity to occupy her body.

====================================

CHAPTER 3

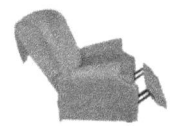

====================================

Chapter - 3 -

What Signals Earthbound Entities?

By making you know they are there with you

This happened one night, while spending the night in an old, cozy and charming little hotel on the Canadian East coast.

In bed, about to fall asleep, in the darkness a white hazy figured appeared in front of them.

Surprised, my friend whispered to her husband "Did you see it?"
In a whisper, her husband said, "Yes."

They froze, not moving, wondering what will happen next.

This happened a few times and then my friend busted into a good laugh.

The white hazy figure would appear each time she was clearing her throat in an attempt to dislodge a broken capsule in her throat – releasing the powdery vitamin within.

No real ghost involved here.

By appearing to you

In my experience, when earthbound entities psychically show themselves to me in bright daylight, they look taller than average, since their ether body floats about 20 centimeters (8 inches) above the ground, or 10 centimeters (4 inches) higher than the place they sit on. This also happens with people still living in the physical world who are thinking intensely about me. In both cases, this happens when they want to tell me something.

In a disturbing clairvoyant dream, I saw a man I knew decide to kill himself. And as usual at that time, I went back into the dream and changed the end of the dream so that he would live. A few weeks later, while I was alone and driving back to my office, the man appeared to me.
He was sitting in the front seat, passenger side, floating about 10 centimeters above the seat. Furious, looking at me, he said, *"How dare did you change my future?"*

Needless to say, I had to do a lot of talking to defend my intervention. ... It was also the last time I went back into a clairvoyant dream to change someone else's future.

By a client during a regular hypnotherapy session

In that case, I only psychically glimpse what is going on from the other-side point of view. I focus only on the well-being of my client, making sure they free themselves of the source of their predicaments and have the cooperation of the earthbound entity to leave the host and go "home."

By a surrogate hypnotherapy session

Explaining a surrogate session is simple. However, to understand it one must experience it. It is a technique I developed in 1986 and teach since the early 1990's.

What is a surrogate? It is a person who represents the client, or a person visiting a building, a place or vacant land.

The contact is direct, with no invoking of "Spirit."

Opening oneself up and invoking "Spirit" is as threatening as playing with the Ouija board.

The Facilitator ensures the authenticity of the session as well the security of the surrogate who connects the Energy field of the subject to contact.

This is "high voltage" work. The maximum is two sessions a day, being the surrogate or the facilitator.

A surrogate (usually a clinical hypnotherapist trained in that modality by me), assisted by a facilitator (also a clinical hypnotherapist trained by me in that modality), contacts the Energy field of an absent person (dead or alive), a building, animals, wildlife, waterfowl tress or an open space they are requested to connect with.

The surrogate – the one who connects the Energy of the subject – goes into a trance and becomes the subject. This allows the surrogate to bypass the brain and connect with the Energy of the subject to investigate and attempt to correct the previously identified issue.

This is psychic detective work at its best. Personally, as a surrogate, having established a deep connection with the subject, I then become a clinical hypnotherapist – helping the *subject* to whom I am deeply connected, while staying an observer. As a colleague stated, it requires awareness, wisdom, knowledge and no thoughts.

To my understanding, in this modality, accessing a multi-conscious awareness that is experienced as only a surrogate can experience it – I learned that our true self, our essence is part of the universe.

There is no privacy in the universe. Since everything is Energy and Energy is everything, by going into a trance with proper training, guidance and preparation, one can *safely* access any information we want about a person or anything else.

In a deep hypnotic trance during surrogate work, attaining a heightened sense of awareness allows subconscious information to come to conscious awareness. One could say we are all hackers!

In my experience, during surrogate sessions I access events that had happened in many languages. Being in a deep trance I psychically connect with my five senses, converse with them, listen to what they express about themselves.
I see, hear, taste, smell and feel what the essence I connected with experienced ... according to them, while staying their hypnotherapist. However, I never paid attention to the language used, since the people, dead or alive, for whom the sessions are requested usually speak English or French.

I performed many surrogate hypnotherapy sessions while at the Hypnotism Training Institute of Alberta campus in Budapest, Hungary. The communication was clear, as usual, as an appointed attendee translated the session in Hungarian to the students in the classroom.

After one of the sessions, my facilitator asked whether I knew he had spoken to me twice in Hungarian during the session, and that I had responded appropriately each time.

"*No, I did not. Did the class notice it?*"

"*Oh, yes,*" was the answer.

As I watched the filmed session two weeks after returning home from my heart-warming trip to Hungary, I could clearly see the facilitator gesturing to the class to pay attention to my response at his suggestions in Hungarian.

It made me realize: *Hold it, the communication was crystal clear, although I do not speak a word of Hungarian, and the spirit of the deceased person as well as the spirits of the people still living I connected with do not understand a word of English.*

And the biblical story of the Tower of Babel and the confusion of tongues came to mind. I have not opened a religious book since I was 18, and yet the story must have made an impression on me. There are several stories about the Tower of Babel. However, they all explain the same thing: the people all had one language and few words. The only way to control people is to have them speak different languages so they will not understand one another.

I thought, *That must be the original sin the Christian religions are mentioning! We are all in our heads, disregarding our intuition, the tuition that comes from within and our connection to the Universal Energy.*

As I explained this to a friend and supplier, he said, "*Anny, it is Eve who tempted Adam.*"

To which I replied, "*No, don't you know it is a man, a Roman emperor who rewrote the Bible?*"

And my friend replied, "*Well, we have to cover our back, don't we?*"

In my experience, during the hypnosis deep-trance surrogate sessions, the psychic communication, regardless of language, is crystal clear—not in words, not in pictures, only in a strong sense of awareness, so strong I can convey the message in spoken words. During surrogate sessions we enter into the universal memory, the universal memory bank, also known as the Akashic Records. How clear the psychic communication is depending on the ability of the surrogate.

What does the universal memory bank look like? That, I do not know. I suppose it depends on one's perception of what it should look like. It could look like a big, thick book, a library, a file cabinet—whatever your fancy. One can compare it to a radio station, where all we have to do is tune in to the bandwidth of the station.

In my experience, I find it interesting that we tune in for only one thing at a time. It is as though we open the file cabinet of the subject to be investigated and take out only one file.

Entering someone else's Energy field requires safety precautions, thus the need for a trained, experienced clinical hypnotherapist facilitator to keep an eye on the surrogate when doing this kind of work. And because we are so far into the universal memory bank when doing this type of work, for safety reasons two surrogate hypnotherapy sessions a day is the maximum, to make sure we stay intact after the experience.

In Neuro Linguistic Programming (usually referred to as NLP) we learn we can establish rapport and access the Energy field of a person by doing exactly the same gestures and movements of a person we want to establish rapport with. Once hooked into their Energy Field, we can then carefully make the person do what we want them to do.

Interesting, is it not?

Wanting to be as slim as a person you see walking in a store? Watch carefully how they walk and hold themselves, and get into the habit of walking and holding yourself exactly like that person you observed. And yes, you will slim down.

However, you could find yourself having some unexpected side effects. Since the way we walk and hold ourselves is a reflection of what is going on inside of us at the subconscious level, by being the reflection of that particular person you also acquire all their physical and emotional illnesses.

As children, walking or having the same manners as one's mom or dad looks cute. But we wonder why some ailments run in the family. To anchor oneself in the Energy of someone else ensures a fierce battle within.

During surrogate hypnotherapy sessions, can we and do we enter the Energy field of someone still living? Yes, there are many requests for this type of work, with no spirit attachment involved. This could easily be the subject of another book.

Do we need permission to do so? No, since no matter what we do, it is the spirit of the person we contact during the surrogate session who either accepts or rejects what has been suggested or done. It is accepted when the soul is calling for help, and rejected when not. For example, there is absolutely no way one can cause someone to fall in love with them through surrogate session. (There are ways, of course, using the brain.)

One can get confirmation of this when doing Reiki, a modality involving laying of the hand energy. When sending healing energy to an absent person, no matter how good our intention, if the person refuses the healing, the energy strongly flies back in our face.

Bypassing the brain, the physical part of us, since a surrogate session accesses only the mind directly connected to the soul, only the soul, owner of the master plan of the life experience, is in control. When within the master plan, the work will be successful. If not, then there is much more work to be done, and we can do it too.

For example, a client wanted to know why her present husband, although kind and gentle, would not speak to her. Still not satisfied by her present husband's elusive answers, the lady requested a third surrogate session.

As I accessed my client's present husband's Energy, I psychically saw him clearly. Leaning at the end of the bookcase in front of me, laughing and with a strong telepathic message, he said, *"Ah, she is at it again, isn't she? Well, I will explain it to you how come I don't say a word to her."* And he did, and yes, I kept it confidential.

By "playing" with the Ouija board

What is a Ouija board? Looking different from the ones we have now, Ouija boards were originally used in China centuries ago as a means of contacting spirits and were called *writing* boards. The present-day Ouija boards (from French *Oui* and German *Ja*) came into existence as a parlor game in Europe in the mid-1800s, when Spiritism and channeling were at the height of fashion. The Ouija board rapidly evolved from a mind reader to a portal of communication with the dead.

Current Ouija boards patented by Parker Brothers consist of a rectangular game board that is covered with a woodcut-style alphabet, the words *yes, no,* and *good-bye,* and the numbers 0–9. Also included with the game is a heart-shaped plastic planchette. The planchette is the pointer that glides over the board under the direction of an earthbound entity and forms comments and replies to questions by pointing out letters, numbers, making messages, and forming phrases.

This method requires caution. Since they are not seen, one has no idea who the entities are who come forth. It is true that it proves life after death. However, the Ouija board accesses only earthbound entities who are sometimes pretending to be the person one of the seekers would like to contact ... to ask advice on many subjects. From what my clients shared with me, these entities first gave excellent advice and, once their prey blindly believed them, gave advice that ruined their lives.

Sometimes the entity who comes forth describes how he or she died, usually with great emotion. This may entice the earthbound entity to attach to an inquiring person (the host) who seems to have empathy for their predicament.

Ever since he had played with the Ouija board as a preteen, one client had been experiencing a very heavy and sad feeling he could escape only by an unhealthy lifestyle. He had been fascinated by the murder of a young boy in the city where he lived. The young, deceased boy my client inquired about with the Ouija board came forth, totally disoriented and stuck in the feeling of being murdered. Over time, my client experienced a strong feeling of empathy for this young boy, and a strong bond formed between my client, who felt sorry for him and wanted to help him, and the murdered boy, who felt my client was a friend that would help him.

Without my client's knowledge, the boy attached to him, making him feel as if he were being strangled each time he felt threatened. My client reverted to an unhealthy lifestyle to withstand the emotions and the hurt of being strangled.

This went on over a period of more than 30 years. At one point, the murdered boy went into a panic while in my office, and my client experienced the feeling of the boy being strangled, yelling, *"I cannot breathe, I cannot breathe!"*

More work had to be done to make the boy leave my client and go through the Light, detaching himself, and to make sure my client stayed intact from that experience.

For some people, a physical sensation

Some clients complain they feel a particular discomfort since a member of the family died, noticing it is the same discomfort that person used to complain about. Some clients know a loved one *is there* by feeling an embrace. It is easy to observe as the person is engaged in a conversation about the defund while caressing a shoulder if though someone is reassuring them. I personally know someone *is there* with my client by a strong physical sensation in my lower legs.

===================================

CHAPTER 4

===================================

Chapter - 4 -

What Happens Once The Physical Body Is Dead?

Clients, colleagues and friends explained how in a near-death experience or in a life-threatening situation, they reviewed their lives in a fraction of a second.

Deceased persons we contacted—usually by accessing the Spirit world through surrogate hypnotherapy sessions—confirmed how, once dead, everything they regretted having done or not done sits heavily on their conscience.

Is there any prevention? Having listened to so many entities at different stages of life or death, from my point of view, the key is to make peace with ourselves.

The many reasons to stay earthbound.

One of the reasons entities stay earthbound is not realizing they have left their physical body. Realizing no one pays attention to them, they are existing and do not have a life, the urge then to attach themselves to a living person.

This usually happens when the person experienced a sudden death, or when so heavily drugged she or he was out of the body before the body actually died. There are, of course, many other reasons, depending on stage of life at death.

John the Banker: Not wanting to leave.

One of my clients attending college explained he had lots of problems with his studies. Very much aware of how he was feeling, my client explained the perception was more related to feelings and power flowing through his body. He had had this feeling since coming back from a summer vacation in Europe with his wife, and he was not quite sure why.

They had gone to some places that actually overwhelmed him with their feeling. He was touching things and he could get a feeling from them—*"you know, bad, good, something happened here"*—and he had entered a lot of places that felt really familiar to him and wondered if that made a whole lot of sense. In Venice, in particular, when touching some walls, he had experienced a lot of bad feelings, and it felt rather strange to him.

"I'm not sure if that's what stuck with me or not, but I know it's been ever since we got back from Europe, I've felt very overwhelmed, very negative.

I get these really bad sensations at the back of my neck, like energy flowing from the stem of my brain, all the way to the front cerebrum, into my eyes and it kind of makes me feel like my head is swimming.

...and that's kind of stopping me from doing things and that kind of causes turning and twisting in my stomach because I get a bad feeling from it.

...and that's stopping me from doing a lot of things and I've had a really negative outlook on things lately as a result of that. Like I'm trying not to be, to be pessimistic about things and that, but it's difficult."

My client, overwhelmed about it all, had done everything to get over it—Reiki, meditating, you name it—to no avail, and was feeling depressed as well, feeling lost. He also reported that lately lights would go out with a flicker and a *ffzzzzzz* sound as he was entering a room. He had to change many light bulbs each time he walked into a room, lights on, and he wondered what this was all about.

The other problem was that, for whatever reason, his memory retention had changed from photographic memory to immediately forgetting what he had just read.

Having started the session with the regular prayers for protection, I reassured my client and asked him to be prepared for anything and to be comfortable with it. Here is what surfaced—or rather, who showed up—as soon as we started the hypnotherapy session.

Feeling annoyed, and overwhelmed, stomach churning, John, a bank owner aged 56, responded to my queries. Work was not going well. He had lost a lot of money, and he felt very disappointed.

Anny: *"For a bank owner, losing a lot of money is not exactly what a bank is for. And I understand very well how you feel, John."*

John the banker had joined my client as he landed in Rome, wanting to help, as my client was feeling worried about the trip.

John was traveling a lot. His main country of business was America. He did not remember much of his personal life, only that his wife was the highlight of his life.

As the session unfolded, John went to the end of his life. At that point he was 62, feeling depressed and desperate.

Banker: *"I am leaving too early. I don't want to leave."*

His body was dead, and he did not want to leave.

Anny: *"Where are you? What is going on?"*

He was in the street, and people were standing around him.

It was embarrassing. *What was embarrassing?*

Banker: *"Everyone saw me that way."*

Although he had never thought about it, John lightened up as I suggested he could be in business again, having his own bank, and with the experience he had gained be very successful at it too.

Much work still had to be done, putting closure to the issue, and helping John go through the Light, and then making sure my client, who had unknowingly been the banker's host, came out of this session intact, feeling free and himself again.

Anybody there?

I had just finished a private hypnotherapy session involving an unpleasant depossession. It was late and cold, and I was tired. My vehicle was parked in the lot behind the office. Loaded down with all I wanted to take home with me in my arms, the steel fire door unlocked but still closed, I pushed on the remote control to open the vehicle's doors and heard an unsettling noise.

Opening the steel door, I could see the vehicle's lights flashing with each loud slam as the doors would unlock, lock, unlock, lock.

Puzzled, I ran to the car with all the lights flashing in rhythm and opened a door as the loud slam indicated the doors were unlocked. With the car still locking and unlocking with loud slams, lights flashing, I put everything I was holding in my arms on the front passenger seat and closed the door, which slammed itself locked, with fanfare.

As I went back into the office to turn off all the lights and set the security system, I leaned against the office fire door, listening to the slamming of the locks. And then I realized what was happening as I was holding my vehicle remote in my hand: the door command button was still pushed down, stuck.

Sorry, no ghost involved here…

The story of Sally: Not knowing her body was dead

A client came wanting to resolve a fear of motorcycles. She was reluctant, as her husband wanted to go on vacation with her riding on the back of a motorcycle he had bought.

She had been aware of some uneasy feelings as a passenger in a car, not as a flyer, and was wondering if this was a control issue, like maybe when not in control of the vehicle, or if it was a trust issue. She had tried to reason it out.

As she was following her husband to work—she driving the car, he on the bike— she experienced a strong feeling of anxiety.

"I wasn't even on the bike, I wasn't near the bike, I was merely following him on the bike. And then, I was, like, okay—this is beyond a trust issue. This goes beyond trust and control. This is something at a deeper level, but I don't know what it is.

I don't really want to go on a bike. But I figure if I'm going to give it an honest try and be on the back, I don't want to be carrying whatever this is with me. I want to get on and just have fun, without having this perceived thought or this memory. I thought let's deal with this right away."

Anny: *"All right. So let's fix it!"*

As I led my client into a hypnotic trance, she explained: *"I see fire. Just a flame and that's it, it's gone. It's gone now, but I feel heavy in my chest."*

As the session unfolded, the information became clearer to my client.

"I see a really bad accident. I'm looking at a car that is just smashed. And it looks like it could have been burnt; it's not black, so it could have been fresh. The accident is fresh. I just see the car. I don't see any flames, but it looks like someone is inside it.

There is something in my chest, between my chest and my throat. Sort of the sensation of somebody having their hands around my throat, like they're choking me, but it's not someone's hands. It's a steering wheel. Somebody got out and walked away. She is standing on the side and does not want to be part of it at all."

At that moment I psychically saw the car. It looked new to me, and heavily damaged, totaled.

Anny to client: "What is her name?"

Sally was 18. She was feeling lonely when she saw my client riding in a school bus. She looked mature, safe and a lot of fun for a grade 10 girl, and Sally decided to attach herself to her. The accident happened 26 years ago. Sally explained she felt scared when crushed in the car.

Anny: "Yes, I would too. And then, Sally, have you ever thought that there is a place where you can go?"

Sally: "Yes."

Anny: "So, what is it that you did not go there?"

Sally: "I don't want to be alone" (crying).

When asked the reason she felt anxiety while following my client's husband on a motorcycle, Sally explained she did not want to get hurt.

As closure was finally made and Sally was willingly leaving my client's Energy field, it was interesting to learn that my client's sore lower back condition went away, as well as the strong feeling of anxiety.

My client later reported she went on vacation, sitting and strapped on the bike back seat and truly enjoyed the ride.

The Lumber Jack: Not knowing where to go.

I do not remember the reason for this surrogate hypnotherapy session. However, I do remember the lumberjack who came forth during that session.

This time, I knew I had to come up with a good reason to get the entity to go through the Light, leaving what was so familiar to him. He was a scruffy lumberjack who had been around for quite some time. He was short, heavily built, unshaven, and walking on snowshoes, with boots with heavy socks coming up almost to his knees.

He wore the typical woolen lumberjack red-and-white checkered shirt, and a long toque with a pompom hanging at the end of a short braided string.

I knew he was a true *bucheron*, a lumberjack from *Les Pays d'En Haut*, The Countries Up There, the way the province of Quebec was called in those days, carrying a heavy axe over his right shoulder.

Convincing him of anything was quite a challenge until I asked him what he had liked the most when he had a body.

The entity brightened up and said: *"Ah, the Montreal red light district! ... You have no idea how good it is after spending months in the bush."*

Knowing entities are very telepathic, as convincingly as I could, and believing my own lies so he would believe me, I explained that there are very good red light districts on the other side of the Light.

Suspicious, he answered: *"Are you sure?"*

Yes, was my answer, *just go there, and if you do not like it up there, you simply do not stay.* And he left as he went through the Light.

From what the entities have taught me, Energy will always assume the image of what or who we believed would appear, just for a time until "waking up," so to speak.

The story of Jodi: The grieving kept her earthbound

Jodi, a 17-year-old young lady, had died in a car accident. Ten years later, her mother was still wondering what happened. Could she have prevented it? Why was her daughter the only one killed in the crash?

Here is a shortened transcript of what the filmed surrogate session revealed.

Anny: *She is there, Jodi is there. And she has a headache like you would not believe. Such a headache that I feel like vomiting. It is that bad a headache. A terrible, terrible, terrible, terrible headache. It is even going down the nape of my neck, the back of my neck.*

(Please note: During a surrogate hypnotherapy session I connect with my five senses when connecting with the subject's Energy field.)

I can feel that here (back of neck). And it is so bad that I feel like throwing up. And my heart is really pounding at the moment.

Anny to Jodi: "*So what is going on, Jodi? What is going on now, Jodi? Come on, what is going on, Jodi?*"

I can start to feel tears. I really want to throw up.

"What is going on, Jodi?"

The way she explained things to me is that *"she is in a dark place at the moment, and she cannot find her way out."* I do not know. She cannot find a way out.

It is almost like she is in a box.

"Jodi, what is keeping you in a box like that? What happened before that? What happened before getting in that box?"

There was a worry. And I can see through a windshield. And I can see a road. It is paved. And I have pain here (places hand on right of abdomen), it is even going down the nape of my neck, the back of my neck. Can I ever feel that here. What is that? And it is so bad that I feel like throwing up. And my heart is really pounding at the moment.
For whatever reason, she shows me a two-lane highway. I have no idea. A two-lane highway. And there are ditches on both sides; it is quite clear on both sides, it is paved.

And she really feels worried. Now I am having a pain here (touching the back of neck, base of skull). She feels worried. She is really worried about something. And she has some gut feelings that are like ... she really does not like it at all.

"What happened, Jodi? What happened?"

Okay, here it goes. She is showing me the side of the road, and there is a kind of a ditch, and whatever she is driving in, she is not showing me the vehicle. All that she is showing me is what she can see. She could see the vehicle going towards the ditch. And I feel like vomiting. Ha, the headache. Everything is black ...

"Jodi, where are you now? Where are you? Where are you, Jodi?"

She said, *"I'm here."*

What is it for that you are still here? You can tell me, that is okay. The only reason this is done, we contacting you, is because we all want you to feel really good about yourself."

(Pause)

For whatever reason, she explained to me that what she had in mind was riding in that vehicle. She was really excited. But then she shows me again, the vehicle going towards that ditch.

"How did it go into that ditch?"

They were following a truck on a two-lane highway, the flying snow blinding what was coming on the other side of the road. As the driver of the vehicle she was in started to pass the truck, I could feel the rush of adrenaline as Jodi, hands holding the dash, thought, *"It is great to be 17!"*

All of a sudden I see another car there, a car coming from the front. According to her it was a big car.
"Jodi, do you know how long that is? ... What is it that you are still here?"

Now, what is interesting is that when I say that ... a face is coming up. And a terrible pain here (touching right side of abdomen). And a face is coming up with bright colors too.

"Who is that, Jodi?"

Now I see a face again, but it is in pastel color. And she said to me, the way, you know she is not talking to me, she just is showing things, and then all of a sudden that odor. There is something about someone having a lot of tears. And I am having a terrible headache again.

"So show me who died?"

Looks like her mother and her grandmother. Lots of tears, lots of tears. And terrible pain. Whoooo.

"Jodi, have you ever thought there is a better way for things?"

By the feel of it she got pretty banged up. "

So okay, let us have a good look here. The headache is coming back.

"Jodi, it has been ten years. How about going on with your life?"

Now I really see the face, I do not know because it is the perception of Jodi, and I see the face very, very close. And the eyes are closed, and I see only one side, this side (right). And a lot of souls there. And from what I can tell myself, from what I see there, because she says very little. She shows me stuff and also make me feel her feelings, is that it is a person that either is the age of her mother now, or at the time was an older person. I have no idea, because it is very much the same, although it is not the same. It looks the same, but then it is not the same.

(I found out later that is was the grieving of her maternal grandmother, one of the persons who is grieving kept her earthbound).

"Jodi, I want you to do something here. Jodi, don't you think it is time to go through that Light? It is your turn."

And here she is standing here in front of me ... she has some hooks all over her, you know that are keeping her, you could say, grounded, so she can go nowhere. And there are lots, and she is showing me that all of these are like weights put on her so she stays grounded. And she is like that (hands out front, palms up), as if to say, *see!*

And she explained that everything is getting much lighter, much, much lighter; from being black in the box there, it becomes quite light.

And the things that are keeping her grounded, so to speak, I find it very interesting, is that the color of her hair when she died, it is a little more on the orangey side ...

"Jodi, do you really want to go?"

"Yes."

Now, what I am doing now, because I want that to be her own doing, I am giving Jodi a kind of a razor. But it is a razor with a blade there, just like the kind that the barbers have. She is smiling when I am saying that.

And then I said, "You are going to shave all those hooks off. It has been 10 years. Shave them off. They are souls of the grieving persons."

And they are all on, either, the highest is at her hip, and they are all down here (motioning from thighs to knees). I am quite surprised, as I am looking at this. ...

"Just shave it off, Jodi. Just set yourself free. You do it, Jodi. It is your journey."

She started here, on my side, yes, on her side there, I suppose (motioning from left hip down to right knee), because they are all here.

She is there in front of me, she starts here at the knee, where she is shaving whoever was attached to her, to the knee here. And then she stopped to look at me, and I said: *"Hey! It is your life. You do what you want. That is right. Now take a deep breath, and as you exhale, do what you want to do."*

My, is she ever quick at removing the rest. Very quick. She is giving me the shaving blade back; she folded and gave it back to me. I said, *"Thank you, Jodi! ... Do you know where the Light is?"*
"Oh," she said, *"over there."*

"How about going through the Light? To a new adventure, a new challenge. And I am going to make a suggestion to you. Please arrange so that next time around, people can enjoy you longer."

You know what? She does not care about that.

"No," her answer is. *"Who wants to be old anyway?"*

"Jodi, what is your reason for saying that? For feeling that way, and saying that way? It is quite a perception of getting older. ... Jodi, where did you get that idea?"

It comes from something she heard about the problems when one gets older. She showed me an ear, the side of the head, and one ear. And it was so clear.

"Well, how about making up your own mind about that?"

"*Oh,*" she said, "*can I?*"

"*Yes, you can. So, Jodi, so what do you want to do now? You know, the Light is there; you can go through it, to start a brand new journey. The choice is yours.*"

And she is gone. What she did—quite a character, that girl—what she did, she put her hands up like that (reaching upwards toward ceiling), made a big jump, and it is almost like diving into that Light. And she is gone. And I feel better... she is gone. Quite interesting, the way she jumped, she just jumped into it, just like somebody diving."

The wrap-up of the session followed, making sure I stayed intact from this experience. Everything was confirmed, such as not wearing a safety belt, and Jodi was the only one who was thrown out of the car and died. The dark place, not knowing her way out, was her having fallen in the ditch face down. This session allowed closure for everyone concerned.

A mother's unfinished business

A lady came for a hypnotherapy session following a dangerous occurrence while driving. With both hands on the steering wheel, she was feeling someone's strong grip on her right hand making her steer to the right and almost creating an accident.

The first private session revealed a mother in a past life wanting to talk and put to rest an issue of long ago. The issue was weighing heavily on her conscience, resulting in my client coming in three times in an attempt to have the mother go through the Light.

During the first and second session, the former mother succeeded at pretending to go through the Light and in fact stayed earthbound. At the third visit, acknowledging the ghost's need to communicate with my client, I suggested to the ghost to stand behind her daughter each time she was riding in the car with her and very gently put her hand on her daughter's shoulder to signal her presence and say what she wanted to say. Since going through the process of sending her mother through the Light twice, I explained to my client she knew how to do it herself. My client called me several weeks later to let me know that after long conversations during car rides, her former mother felt at peace and agreed to leave and get on with her life.

The possessive wife

One day, I received an alarming call from a clinical hypnotherapist and colleague trained with me in surrogate work as well as in dealing with entities living where ghosts are roaming. She was feeling sick and tired, a most unusual situation for her.

In a deep trance, checking my colleague's Energy field, I discovered a big dark grey blurb form attached to my colleague's back, with glaring yellow eyes and the teeth firmly planted in her neck; the other side of the bulky form was almost in the shape of stubbed tail. I found out later that this is the way the ether body appears when the entity is heavily drugged at time of death.

After psychically yanking the form from my colleague's back and having no idea what that was about, the best course was to enclose the form in a thick glass-walled cage until further notice.

Entities taught me that when connecting in the Energy field, we are able to manifest anything of the same wave length or vibration of the spirit world, and whatever we build is solid to them. This is the reason the spirit was stuck in the glass cage I had manifested.

The next move was to connect with whoever that was via a surrogate hypnotherapy session. Having taken all the necessary measures to ensure my facilitator's as well as my own safety, I contacted the entity again. This time she showed herself as an overweight lady wearing a flowery dress, pounding furiously on the glass walls of the cage I had put her into, wanting to get out to beat up my colleague.

Calming her down, I asked the entity to explain her concern. It was about the love her husband and she had for each other, as well as her love for her very young children, and here is what she said.

"We were close and everything, I got the man and the children that I wanted from him, and then that woman removed me from him!"

Anny: *"Look at you, where is your body now?"*
As the recorded session unfolded, here is what I learned. Realizing she had died and had left her body left her speechless and in shock. Heavily drugged, she felt good and had not felt her short illness. She was already out of her body prior to leaving it, her focus totally on her children's well-being. She was still making sure they were dressed properly, the whole thing. Very devoted, she was still really looking after them. Because of their very young age, the children could see her, the reason they never grieved the death of their mother.

Anny: *"That your husband does not love you or anything is not the point. It is: life is for the living."*

"*I'm living!*" was her answer.

Anny: "*Yes, but you have no life. You do not have a body. And you know, it was nice for you to stay around like that, because the children do not even know you are dead. However, there will be a time when they realize you are. So for that, you have to start giving them their space. Because they are getting older.*

"*Have you ever thought that if you would go through the Light, from up there, from above, the inspiration you could give your children would be of much, much higher quality? You would feel better about yourself too?*"

Anny: "*What was the highlight of your life?*"

She said, *when she hooked her husband good!*

Anny (laughing): And she showed me how she did it, and I am not going to explain it.

"*This is private, right?*"

After much work done to effect closure for the good of everyone concerned, I asked if I could open the door and give her a hug. As she looked at me in surprise, I explained she was a good lady who did not know she died.
I opened the door, and she was standing there hesitant until I said, "*Come on. Let me give you a hug. You are quite a lady, aren't you?*"

As I am walking her slowly toward the Light, my arm around her shoulders, I asked if there was anything she wanted to convey to her husband before she went though the Light.

Smiling, she explained, not knowing she was supposedly dead, she was snuggling with him in bed every night, telling him everything she wanted to tell him, especially when he was sleeping, making sure he could feel her. And then, whispering in my ear, she added, *"That is how come there is no other girlfriend!"*

Much more work had to be done before she finally agreed to go through the Light, feeling at peace.

A ghost at the rescue of a dying baby

I had a clairvoyant dream advising me that a friend of mine was about to give up and wanted to die. This was out of character.

Without my friend's knowledge, and wanting to know her reason for wanting to die, a surrogate hypnotherapy session was held and revealed that as my friend was dying at birth, a female earthbound entity attached herself to her, full of compassion, sharing her own energy to the dying newborn to help her live.

What happened next is a classic. The earthbound entity ended up influencing my friend to the point she was reliving the earthbound entity's life. I could see the earthbound entity, a plump single mother, scrubbing the blue stone in front of a front door, the cobblestones of the sidewalk, the street.

She was working very hard as a cleaning lady, with only one goal in mind: to be able to pay her son's tuition so he could have a trade. This was her mission, her goal. She died shortly after her son graduated.

A plump single mother herself, my friend had replayed the ghost's life, working very hard to give her son access to the best education in the trade of his choice, and at the time of the clairvoyant dream, her son was about to graduate from a trade school.

The earthbound entity was sent through the Light, and my friend kept on living.

During a telephone conversation with my friend two weeks after the surrogate hypnotherapy session, I voiced my pleasure at hearing her voice, since I had had a premonition about her dying. To my surprise, she explained that even her son had suspected something and had mailed her a very nice card expressing his love for his mother.

What are the signs of the presence of a ghost?

There are so many signs, I wonder what to explain. The most important is to analyze the situation we find ourselves in, since looking at things emotionally may distort the way we perceive things. Feeling uncomfortable while reading this type of material also signals there is somebody there.

To sum it up, it is important to be aware of what is going on with ourselves and in our immediate surroundings. Being observant is one solution, as you will understand reading the following story.

The lady whose father had passed away: TV changing channels

I was in a bookstore when a lady who had attended one of my presentations, "Things That Go Bump in the Night," started to talk to me about a new situation at home. Stating that her very pious father, who had passed away, had attended church every day, she had started to do the same, although she had seldom gone to church prior to his passing.

She also found it very funny that the TV was changing channels by itself. While she sat on the couch watching a program, the channel would change to sports. Thinking it was the remote control not working properly, she would get up and put the channel back to the program she was watching; and as she was walking back to the couch, the television program switched again to the sports channel

Waiting and wishing they arrive: Feeling uncomfortable

There are many stories of soldiers back from Vietnam. The Vietnam War left deep wounds in the United States.

During my training in exorcism, giving examples of how one can be possessed, the instructor explained how a field radio operator who was posted where a military plane was to land had lost contact with the plane. He knew several soldiers in the plane and waited a long, long time, hoping to get radio contact again. Unknown to him, the plane was shot down and everyone aboard died in the crash. Back from Vietnam and feeling not himself, uncomfortable with his thoughts, his feelings and his health, the military field radio operator sought therapy sessions.

When the plane had crashed, the now disembodied friends of the field radio operator, guided by his wondering where they were and wishing they would arrive, had all gone straight to him and attached themselves, responding to his wish they would arrive

The Story of Marianne: Getting sexually aroused for no apparent reason

As you read the partial transcript of this surrogate hypnotherapy session, you will realize how true it is that living where ghosts are roaming, these disembodied entities are still how they were at time of death. During a surrogate hypnotherapy session, the past unfolds in front of us as if it were today.

Richard, a client, kept feeling a girl around him, although his work did not leave him time for enjoying a relationship. During a surrogate hypnotherapy session, having connected with the Energy of my client, I realized this was a possession, as something appeared out of a very old clock attached to a building and went into my client, possessing her lover from a past life, as it turned out.

Anny: *"Hello, come on, that is okay, I saw you.*

I saw you! Are you ever a very, very good-looking woman! Come on, just get out from behind him. Just get out of there, because I can see you. I can see your dress. Your arms now, and I see you are beautiful. I want to see you completely!"

She is a very young lady, I mean not a child. A lady in her twenties, early twenties.
I am not good with history, so I do not know, but she has also a very nice hat on. It is a hat that goes around the head, not something that is sitting on it; it is enveloping the head. It is quite a fancy thing. There is a kind of a visor on top of it in those days, and it is really nice up front. It is almost like a bonnet, but a very fancy one. That is a bonnet that a person would wear to be dressed up. And the fabric is white with some flowers, and she is smiling at me.

Now she has a cut almost low in the front of her dress and then she has a ... (I could not explain it) *it is quite ...* because of that it is quite narrow on the shoulders, and then has long sleeves. And it is gathered, like this, you know (gesturing), and then it gets tighter around the forearm, it gets tighter, and then there is a cuff there with a little thing around it. I am not sure what you call it in English. Anyway, that is really nice. And then it is quite molded, the bust, and it is a big, long dress.
Anny: *"My, are you ever pretty! This is wonderful, you look absolutely gorgeous. Yes, and what are you doing here?"*

And now I see the street and the houses. It is in Europe, that comes from Europe. Because it is like, we would call it in Canada, row houses. But in fact it is not; that was what we call here townhouses; and I can see the street, the cobblestones, and then I can see the sidewalks, very narrow sidewalks.

Anny: "How could you walk on that with your dress so wide?"

She laughs, and I can see the houses; they are all bricks. And also, bigger than bricks, what you call stones. Very pretty.

Anny: "Well, what are you doing here? You see me, don't you?"

"Yes, I see you. I like that guy."

Anny: "You do?"

She said: "Yes!"

Anny: "Oh, you like him?"

She said: "Yes, I do."

Anny: "What is it about him that you like?"

Now she is putting—she is quite a flirt! —she is putting her arm around Richard's Energy, and said: "You know, it was a secret . . . we used to be lovers!"

Anny: "Is that right? How long ago?"

I see those houses again, and the street, and at the end of the street there is a kind of a plaza. Place in French, it was quite nice.

She said: "It was a secret."

Anny: "Is that right? How come?"

She is showing me a drawing of my client, the way he used to be. Oh, it was at the time when the men had the lower part of the legs very tight, very, very tight in what they were wearing.
And she said: "He was as handsome then as he is now."

Anny: "Is that right? So what are you doing here?"

"I found him," she said.

And she is flirting, let me tell you, what a flirt (laughing).

Focusing on the Energy of my client, I asked: *"How do you feel, Richard?"*

Richard, whom I was connecting with during the surrogate hypnotherapy session: *"Well, I felt a flirting girl!"*

Anny: "Do you know who made you feel that way? ... It is her."

Richard: "It is her?"

Anny: "Yes, because you are her man."

And I can feel the arousing, by the way, it is very interesting. Yes, she is quite a flirt.
Anny: "Yup!"

Mm-hmm. The arousing is something else. I said, okay, I am asking her name by telepathy ... and she keeps ... I do not know if that makes any sense, but she is called Marianne.

Anny: "Marianne?"

"Yes, my name is Marianne." ... "Well," said Marianne, "have a look."

She is showing me how he used to look, what he used to wear. Of course, he was very handsome, just like now.

Anny: "Yes, and the same face too, and the same body."

Marianne: "Mm-hmm."

Anny (laughing): "Okay, excuse me, I find it cute. The thing is that, Marianne, have a look at how he was dressed at the time. What he was wearing. And look at what you are wearing."

Marianne: "A pretty dress."

I said: "It is rather pretty. The thing is, I would like you to observe what is he wearing now. Pay attention. And I would like you to have a look at the ladies in the same age as you, what they are wearing now."

"Well," she said, "this is disgusting. There is nothing nice about it."

Anny: "Just a moment! This is how things are now."

She is confused now, and she said: "Just a moment here."
Anny: "We are in another time, another life. Have a look at the streets ..."

Well, she does not want to go away from Henry. She calls him Henry. So, she must be from when they knew each other; he was not Richard then. But she is familiar with Henry, not with Richard, so she must be from a country of that area, when the whole thing happened.

She looked at me and said: "We are from Holland."

That is it. Fine, as she shows me again that street, those houses, and that beautiful plaza.

Anny: "Marianne, did you notice that you can go through the wall if you want to, through doors and everything, even through Henry?"

She said, "Yes."

Anny: "It is because you are in another dimension. Henry has a physical body; you don't."

Marianne: "What?"

Anny: "What I am saying to you is this, I see you because I am doing this type of work, but he does not. And when you attach yourself to him the way you are, when you started, it makes him feel odd. He is confused."

"Well," she said, " he should not, he knows me."

Anny: "Just a moment. You are in another time. In another life. It is another time. Another life. So, I would like you to go back to when you had a body, because you do not have one now."

Marianne: "Yes, but it is great, I go though things, and I found him. I like that clock you saw first, so I stayed with that clock a long time, but I never did anything. But when I saw Henry again, the love of my life ..."

Anny: "And you likely were the love of his life, weren't you?"

Marianne: "Yes."

Anny: "So I would like you to go back to when you knew each other. Tell me what was happening there? I would like you to go back to just before you died."

Marianne: "What do you mean?"

Anny: "I said, just before your body was not alive anymore. Oh, yes. Go back there ..."

I can see ... it is quite interesting what I see. I cannot believe what I am seeing here.

She was attacked. She was coming back with a basket that she was holding with some food in it. She was walking on the street. And she was in an area that she was not familiar with, walking there. And I can feel the chills, I can feel the goose bumps all over her body, as all of a sudden, a bunch of men arrive with big clubs, sticks, quite heavy. A whole bunch, there were six.
They came from ... she did not know where. And came towards her, and she was, oh, I can feel it, my whole body there (gesturing). And they clubbed her to death. To death. To get what was in that basket. And she had the dress on that she has now.

Anny: "Well, Marianne, I must say that you made a nice job at having that dress cleaned and nicely pressed and whatever you did in those days."
She said: "Thank you!"

Anny: "Because I see the way that dress was when they were finished with you."

Marianne: "Yes, I got up."

She said she started to put her dress back on. And she walked away.

Anny: "Hold it, turn around. Look at you there."

Marianne: "That's me!"

Anny: "Yes, and that is you here, and that is you there now."

Marianne: "Yes."

Anny: "Now, go back at that time. And this time I would like you to look up. Do you see that Light?"

She said yes, and because she had that basket with things, she wanted to deliver it. She had to, so she went, but this time she ran, and for whatever reason, she said those guys did not run after her. She ran and got into a house and deposited the basket and ran out right away.

Anny: "Is that right? Have a look up again. Did you notice that Light?"

Marianne: "Yes."

Anny: "Now that the basket has been delivered, have you ever thought of going through that Light? "

Marianne: "No." *Because she believed in God, and God did not show up, so she did not go anywhere. She had no idea how God looked like.*

Anny: "Well, that's because you have to go through that Light to see God. Mm-hmm."

Leaving the love of their life of so long ago was not easy to do for either of them. Wrapping it up, much work still had to be done before we could end this session, leaving them both strong, at peace, and in their personal time in the moment.

======================================

CHAPTER 5

======================================

Chapter - 5 -

Ghosts In Houses, Buildings And Land

A company in Europe dealing in real estate discovered the reason a nice, cosy-looking mansion on a beautiful estate was for sale at a very low price. It was impossible to spend the night there, as ghosts were making themselves seen and heard. They were monks still fiercely fighting for their lives, loudly defending their place as they were murdered, and chasing everyone out of what used to be their cloister.

A cultural belief

On one occasion, I was contacted to check what was going on at a newly developed resort in Canada. I discovered that spirits of former occupants considered this land theirs and had decided to chase the occupants away by creating accidents.

The alarming situation, a child almost run over on the resort, made the owner call us for help. Believing their duty was to stay earthbound to defend their blood brothers and sisters, and unconvinced to move on, they made a deal in exchange for peaceful occupancy.

Following the ancestors' instructions, a monument made of stone was built at the entrance of the resort, with an engraved metal plate acknowledging the ancestors who had occupied the land long ago.

In some cultures, the elders believe they must stay around after they die to help the living ones and retain their traditions, and they do. The traditions usually involve lands where they roamed and lived a very long time ago.

The new restaurant on the lake shore

In one situation, a surrogate hypnotherapy session was requested to find out what was causing total chaos in a newly built restaurant. At night doors would slam shut and things would fall off the shelves, and part of the restaurant would turn ice cold in spite of the thermostat set at an unusually high temperature.

One evening at closing time, while the assistant manager was clearing the tables, the assistant manager heard something, and as he turned around, he saw that a table he had just cleared was still set up. The restaurant was closed from Saturday night and reopened on Monday morning.
Coming to work on a Sunday, the assistant manager could hear loud footsteps and thought someone had entered the restaurant. Another time the manager who was the first to return to work on Mondays found a candle still burning on a table.

A big beaver who was wrecking the marina kept being killed, only to reappear alive, still wrecking the marina. It was obvious someone did not want them there and was giving an uncomfortable feeling to anyone who would enter that space.

The restaurant was located on a lake shore in an idyllic part of Canada. It faced the beautiful, impressive Lesser Slave Lake. Facing the restaurant, the marina could be seen on the left, with Lesser Slave River discharging onto the lake a little farther off. We have gorgeous late summers in Canada, and this was a day like that. From the landscape and from the impressive forest of pine trees, one can see this is the northern part of Alberta. As I learned during the surrogate session, ghosts of the inhabitants who used to live on the other side of the lake had taken on the mission of defending the land where the restaurant had been built, the very place where a group of bands would meet once a year to discuss battle strategies as well as where to find an abundant food supply.

As soon as I entered a deep hypnotic trance, I found it quite interesting that at one side of me there were some spikes, just as if my aura wanted to defend itself from something. It was quite interesting.

And I can see now, ah! I see a man standing there.

I can see the property from above and I am coming from the side. Very much like one of the pictures, where I can see the arm—well it is not an arm, it is like something is entering the land, like an arm, where all the boats can dock. Well, not dock, where the boats get shelter, so to speak. It is a marina.
And then I see the rest there, at the point, near the water. Seeing it from above, the marina has the shape of a hockey stick: a straight flat stick with a wide blade to catch things on the ice.

And the man there. He is very clear, and he is quite powerful. Very impressive. He has in front of him a breast panel, something quite fancy made of porcupine quills, like something attached to his garment in front of him on his chest. It looks like two rows of horizontal porcupine quills on top of his chest, the white on the front, and black towards the side of his chest, with two porcupine quills in the middle to mark a separation between the two rows.

He has a bright head, he is looking at me, on the face he has some paint. He has something on his head. It is a war bonnet. But on his forehead there are feathers. The eagle feathers are standing straight up. The feathers are some on a point, and some on the side, and also something attached to the bonnet that are falling, almost covering each ear.

He is very intimidating. A very impressive-looking man. I can see him looking at me. He is the chief. He is in front of me, and I can see that it is not winter yet. The water from the river discharging into the lake is running quite smooth. And I am looking, and I can see the property and the chief. I do not know from what tribe he is.

And he is looking at me, and I am asking him what is it that makes him feel the way he feels about that beautiful property.

It is the land of his people. There is something about ancestors. And he looks so intimidating. He is saying it is their land. It is their land. It is theirs.

"Well," he said, "look," as he is gesturing to the other side of the lake. All of a sudden, I see a lots of tepees there. That is where they are settling for the winter.

I say, "Well, they are not there anymore. As a matter of fact, if you look around, not many Canadians live in tepees anymore."

He is insisting that it is their land.

"The thing is, it is no longer your land."

He said they really liked it there.

And I said, "I can understand that. That is the reason the person that bought that piece of property put in such a beautiful restaurant there. Don't you see that someone thought so much about that piece of property that they thought of developing it like that?"

As I am listening to him, we are talking about the land. I can see his tepee there, the children running around. But that was a long time ago. And tepees and the women. And more tepees and the women. This was a very big tribe. I can see horses dragging travois behind them. A very, very long time ago. He says to me it was such a good place, when they died, they all decided to stay there.
I explained, "Well, once you died, that is no place to be."

He says, "Well, wait a minute! It is a good place to be!"

I said, "Don't you see the Light up there? The Light is there, the land is here. The Light is very beautiful at the top. The thing is, don't you want to nourish your spirit?"

He said, yes, that is what they do. They stay on the property and they nourish their spirit.

I said, "To nourish your spirit you have to go to that Light over there! Yah."

"Well," he says, "the spirits are like that. This is our land, so we are staying on the land. We like the land, so we are staying on it." He said the spirits stayed with the land.

Something is going on about the Light. It is over there, it is a shaft of Light coming down and unfolding itself.

"If you really like the land, walk on the path of the Light and take everybody with you, go through the Light, you can come back in a body, in your own body, with your own body, so that you can see everything for the land that you love."

He said, "Okay."

You know, from the way he is dressed, I am really wondering what time period it is. A hundred fifty to two hundred years ago, maybe even much longer than that. You should see his face. Painting, black, some white. ... And what he is wearing is made of animal skin. He smiles as I am describing him.

"What can we do so that you are happy and the people who are on this property? So that there is happiness for the owners, just like you want to be happy?"

The chief explains his people would be proud if there was an wooden statue to the like of him carved out of a local tree. He is insisting it should be a true representation of his band, with the face painted with the right color, the war bonnet, and the black-and-white porcupine-quills panel on the chest.

I said, "I don't know if that will be possible, to find someone who could carve it. I am going to convey the message to the present owners of the land and let them figure it out."

And he is showing the space between the main entrance of the restaurant facing the parking lot. And he is showing me where he would like to have it stand.

"The thing is, it is not a good idea. There are birds. You know what birds do when they perch on something."

He said, "I never thought about that."

So he said, "Maybe something drawn."
I make a sketch that I think he may like, and he did.

"Okay, I will convey that."

He says, "Something that looks like me. I want it to be correct. Porcupine quills, the headpiece, the paint on my face. Have it there, and a kind of a little roof over it to protect it from the weather and from the birds too."

"The thing is that," he says, "it is all about the people who lived on this land. Honor. Long before you. Honor the people who inherited this land long before you."

I explain to him that I will be able to make it with a sketch. And he explained how he wanted it to be. Okay. Now.
(Long pause)

"I will convey that to the owner, but then I require some cooperation from you. I require you to help me so I can help you. So, okay—that shaft of light is still there, and obviously you are a head figure. How about directing your people to step into that shaft of Light? So that they can, once they go through the Light, they can get their own body and be useful to the land in any way they choose, as long as it is useful to the land and to this beautiful country. And make sure it is peaceful."

He laughed when I said "peaceful." I said, "Yes, peace, peace."

He is gathering all the people—they are folding their tepees—gathering the children. They are folding their tepees.
"Yes, take your horses with you, the whole thing."

I am asking the chief to make sure everybody goes through the Light, make sure they go all through the Light—men, women, children. The tepees, the horses, everything. The whole thing.

(Pause)

The whole thing. It is huge. And the shaft of Light is going up now.

"How did you fit everybody in there? On that piece of property?"

Now everybody is going through the Light, except the chief. I am asking everybody to go through, and I am asking him to make sure that all the spirits in that place are going through.

And now I want him to take a look at that place, how beautiful that place is, how the people who built it built something that is an honor to the land. It was an honor to the land that they built something so beautiful.
And how about doing something so it is pleasant to be in that building? And that everybody that works in that restaurant is extremely happy. An honor to the land where it is built.

I am asking him also to use his power and that he does something to the land; it is very special. For his people, so that the land is protected. He is giving me something. It looks like he is holding ashes in his hand. Ashes of a certain bark of a tree. And it is for protection, good luck, harmony and a good promise. And he is carefully putting it in a leather pouch, and giving it to me with instructions on how to use it.

Anny to Facilitator: *So, anything else?*

Facilitator: *"There is a name?"*

Anny: *"Yes, there is, and I cannot pronounce it."*

Not that long ago he never thought someone will contact him. I am smiling as the shaft of Light is coming down there again, inviting. The people who are now on that land love it. They are taking very good care of it. You can go and join your people.

All of a sudden, he has a pipe. He is presenting me a pipe. It is his own pipe. It has a long and straight wooden stem, with a kind of a bowl, very narrow where it is attached to the wood stem and looking like a cut-down miniature barrel at the top where something is put in to be lit and smoked. The wood stem and the barrel are black and shiny from being held. This pipe must have been used for a very long time.
He is presenting it to me, holding the end in his left hand and his right hand holding the pipe at the barrel. It is his own pipe and I am humbled by the present. He is getting very tired now.

"You deserve to go into that Light. How about stepping into that shaft of Light? I know you love that land. It is time now to let someone else look after it with great care."

And he left.

Using the ashes as instructed, I started with the kitchen, and I am having that energy radiate through the restaurant, through the window panes, and start to expand itself all the way back, the whole thing. Expanding, expanding. And then also raise up both sides of the building, and the walking path. Just like flushing out negativity and welcoming happiness, peace and good luck. Something like a fountain, you know, the fountains that are low, and then raised and raised, and then it is over the roof? The property seems quite clear now, and I am doing something so that it stays clear. So that it stays clear. And putting an enjoyable feeling.

Now looking at the energy of the building itself. The energy of the building is matching the energy of the evergreen trees. The energy of the trees and the energy of the building are bonding. It is beautiful to see. I find it extremely interesting that the energy of the building has improved in such a distinctive way.

The situation resolved, the restaurant started to function as it should, pleasant, experiencing a very good business. It has been ten years since this session was requested. As I was copying the transcript of this session, I gave a copy to an elder for his views on the tribe of so long ago.
The most humbling experience was the explanation of receiving the chief's pipe. It was explained that to give me that pipe the chief must have regarded me with the highest esteem, since a pipe bearer is someone who is highly respected and consulted for guidance. The elder who is a friend of mine recommended I get in contact with a First Nations woman pipe bearer, explain this event and ask her to find my own pipe.

Since then, I have learned that the pipe I was given by the Chief is a very old pipe, probably four hundred years old. It was obvious to me that something other than tobacco was smoked in that pipe. The pipe was black with a long straight stem, very different from all the pictures in dictionaries.

Wishing I could see a drawing of the headpiece, the war bonnet the chief was wearing, feather straight up, something hanging over his ears, I found out the straight-up headdress was originally Blackfoot and was worn by both men and women. The headdress was fashioned with eagle feathers standing straight up. Winter weasel pelt was attached to the headband, hanging around the neck, covering the ears explained what I had observed hanging around the neck.

So far, it is the first and only time I have seen a shaft of Light unfolding itself from the sky, ready to lift up whoever had stepped into.
About the communication. It is only dawning on me now that although I did not speak the chief's language, our communication was crystal clear.

As I am realizing all this, although the focus was to have peace in the land and the restaurant of that area, I wish I had asked more questions about that tribe, one including how and where did they died. Why had such a big band decided to stay together, and what made them settle for the winter in this idyllic Lesser Slave Lake area?

An interesting case was the energy stuck in lumber that used to be part of a building where dishonest activities had taken place before the building was torn down. The use of this lumber resulted in psychically polluting the new premises, with interesting results, making it very difficult to conduct business in that particular strip mall. Once the energy cleared and good and pleasant energy infused the lumber, business started to flourish.

Schaeffer the gambler

Of all the surrogate hypnotherapy reading sessions performed to clear a building, the following transcript of a session is the most entertaining one I have done so far. In spite of everything he had done, a landowner could not lease one end of a strip mall he had recently bought. For whatever reason, nobody could enter one end of the building.

As you read this, you will understand why I left the transcript of the session almost intact. The complete session took about one hour. As in all the stories, some editing has been done to respect the privacy of the people involved.

As I was bringing the picture of the building to mind, facing the bay that could not be leased, I felt something preventing me from entering the building.

I am looking at the building and there is, like, an energy that does not want anybody to come close. And it is the door, there is something about the door.

So, I am having a sense here (gesturing), and as I am, I am approaching the door. There is something about that door there. It is like ... like a magnetic field, you could say, that makes it, like, don't even go near there.
I want to go in there, but there is, like, a magnetic field that prevents me, so I suppose it prevents anybody, to get in there that it does not want to. So as I am looking at this, I can psychically see a magnetic field. It is, like, half a saucer or half a plate that is up front, at that door.

There is something about that door there. So, as I am looking at the door the magnetic field is like ... my God, I have a scratchy back and head all of a sudden with that. ...

So, what happened is that I am starting to have goose bumps in my left leg and my left body; it is moving up as I am looking at this.

You know the old type of records, where you could see the grooves, well, it looks like something like that, half of it, is in front of that door, and the grooves send a magnetic field that would prevent anybody from going in there. I wonder where that comes from. I find it very interesting, and that shiver is on my left side. It is interesting, and I want to get into that building.

I am in front of the building. It is at my left side. The place that I am now facing is the left side as I am facing it. I am finding it very interesting that now my left eye has started to water. There is something about it.
Okay, just a moment there; it is almost like the building is, like, an entity by itself and half of it is paralyzed, because of my eye starting to water; it was like there is no control, no control. So, my left eye is starting to water just like there is no control; my left side of the body, it is a funny feeling, almost like it is numb, paralyzed.

It is paralyzed, so as I am looking at the building there is something, and is it ever coming strong now. Something is paralyzing that side of the building. So, as I am facing it, it is the left side as I am facing it. There is something that is paralyzing the whole side.

So where does that come from? Where does that come from?

Totally paralyzed. So, I do everything to get inside of the building, and as I want to force myself inside the building, I have a kind of a pain, that now, before my left side was kind of goose-bumped, now it is paralyzed.

Starting to have shoots of pain there (gesturing), from behind my knee, my thigh really, the back. It is a sharp pain now, almost like ... I don't know. And also from my elbow to my shoulder; it is a very sharp pain too. I find that extremely interesting, and it is getting extremely, extremely uncomfortable. And my eye feels like, I don't know if it does, but it feels like there is less and less control. So there is something there.
My facilitator is now instructing me to strengthen my own Energy field to make sure I stay intact from this adventure and allow me to walk inside the building and just be an observer of what is going on inside.

Anny: All right. There is something on the left side of the building.

There is absolutely something on that side. I am starting to walk inside of the building, and the pain shoots again, but this time only my leg from my knee, but it is the back, where I am seated, and it is like, ... oh, oh.

Okay, something is going on in that building. ... What is it? ... What is it?

I am aware of a big pool of blood. ... A big pool of blood. ... A very big pool of blood. It is a mess. There must have been a gunfight to bring the place the way it appeared to me.

I am seeing now, someone—you could call it a ghost, spirit, whatever. I am seeing someone there, sitting there, near that pool of blood. He is sitting on the floor, cross-legged. Sitting there, looking at me.

Anny: What do you do there?

Something happened there. And by the looks of it, it happened a very long time ago. Very, very long time ago.

A Tarot card that keeps coming to mind and it is the card of the—I usually can tell the name—it is the disc, and I see a Tarot card disc. A Pentacle.

Pentacle, yes, and he is there, and it is like the Pentacle man; there is one Pentacle with a man only, but there he is; for whatever reason, he got stomped on. He got crushed, so that the proportions are wrong. And it is almost like he got crushed, half of himself, so it is like he is wider. It is like, according to him it pushed on him, so for whatever reason, that is what he shows me. It is a Pentacle, and it looks like he is the man in the Four of Pentacles, leaning against a beam, holding a big Pentacle on his chest.

It has something to do with work. I find it very interesting that it shows itself as a Tarot card. ... It is the Four of Pentacles, and it has something to do with work.

I am looking at him, and I said, "What do you want to tell me?"

He wants to tell me it is his place. He used to work there, and it belongs to him.

There is something about that building, that place where he stands, where he's crushed. The Four of Pentacles, it is his place, it belongs to him, he used to work there. Pentacle is money, and so what is going on here? What is going on here?

Something very heavy came loose, as he was working, and it fell on his head. I can see it. It is a kind of a chandelier. It was a huge wooden chandelier made in the shape of a wagon wheel and holding big, wide candles, not the fancy ones, nor gracious. Very old, the way they hung those things in a pub. Two of the six steel chains holding the heavy chandelier got cut in a gunfight, crashed, and fell on him. Bullet traces were proof the gunfight must have gone on for a while, with blood all over the place. Clothing still dangling from the chandelier half up, hanging from the remaining four chains. That is a long time ago, by the way.

Remembering the reason this session was done, I am asking that entity or whatever Energy that is, would he be happy if there was prosperity in that building again? Would he be happy if business was good again in there? How about cleaning up the place?
He is looking at me as if to say, "Hmm, let's think about that."

Anny: What was going on in this place?

"Gamble."

Anny: Ha ah! (laughing).

He was gambling, and he was very good at it. By the looks of it, he was not being honest about it, either. He was a professional gambler. And a professional gambler wins! It was very exciting, very profitable too, that is why the Pentacle. Mm-hmm! Gambling, doing very well by the way, but then, well. ...

Okay, I would like to do something so that the entity knows that, you know what, if he wants to gamble, and do very well, how about going through the Light, where he is going to do his thing?

Facilitator: "Has he told you his name?"

He says it was depending on who was calling him (laughing). And he is laughing, and people did not even know it was his building, but by golly, that was his! Lots of money, so he was pretending that he was just working in there. But in fact, he was the owner of that gambling place. Okay, so now, how about cleaning up all that so that the owners now can make pretty good money with that thing, the way he did, really?

After all, fair is fair. You know, the way the chandelier fell, or whatever it was, it was something very heavy hanging on the ceiling—it crushed, really, it banged him almost on the face, half of it, gave him quite a blow, and it is the left side that got really, really banged up, although he was crushed completely. So now, okay. I am readjusting his limbs, the leg, for him; it is his right leg because I am facing him. Okay, because I was mirroring him, so now I am putting things back together there. And I am readjusting his clothes. The thing is, he is strange, because he is dressed like the guy, the Four of Pentacles. He is a weasel.

He laughs. He said:

"You have to be, because when you are down, and you want to win, you have to be a weasel."

And he was pretty good at it. Okay, so now ... he is stretching himself out, upright. He is getting back to his height. And the pain completely subsided, completely subsided. The pain in my leg and my forearm. Completely subsided now. My left eye is still like no control over it, but I know that is simply the impression I am having at the moment. So now I am asking him how about getting some buckets of water and cleaning up the floor? Mopping it up. That is enough. Enough is enough.

Okay, it is going very well, we are doing it together. I am helping him. So, hmm, looks pretty good, huh? He is checking everything, as we work together. And he is taking things, you could call it, out of the woodwork. There was a lot going on in that building when he was there!
So now we are going to go out through the front door. And there is that energy thing there, and we better do something about it.

All what he wants to take with him is still inside, in front of the door. There is a lot of boxes and he is a good packer, let me tell you.

So now, I am asking him: "Is it all right if we open the door and put some fresh air in there, some new energy? Well, you know, you are going to go to a place where you can bring all your stuff, so how about doing it, putting all your stuff outside the building. And there is that magnetic thing outside the door, and we will see what will do with it after."

Okay, you should see the big boxes.

According to him, what would clear the whole place? He has a bottle, a bottle that is shaped almost like a cone. And there is a sprayer on top of it with a kind of a cord; a tube at the end of it is like a pump. It is quite big; you could say it is like a one-liter bottle, no, a liter and a half. But it is cone-shaped; it is not white, it is clear. The outside is sanded, and it is clear, and he put a special thing in there, and he is following me as I am using that thing to squeeze and spray the whole building inside.

As I am asking, what is that thing inside the bottle that does that, and he says, it is something special that he likes to remove the odor of mildew. And I am going there, it is quite something, the contraption. And he shows me to do that, do that. Pretty good, boss! Okay, so now, huh, so I will squeeze, I will squeeze, I will squeeze.

All right, so now there is still some in the bottle; he said, "That is okay." Not much, about five centimeters (two inches) left in the bottle.

So now, he is opening the door. And he is looking at all the stuff, all the boxes. You could call it moving boxes, but in those days, they did not have those type of boxes. And they are tied with rope, to keep everything safely inside each box, and he is looking at all the boxes that he put on that magnetic field outside. He put it in there. And he says to me,

"Did you know that the edge of the magnetic field is like a fence? You cannot pass."

Anny: "You can believe it, you cannot pass. I experienced that!"

Gambler: "Oh well, that is an old trick I learned a long time ago".

When asked how come the owner of the building, who is a very good dowser, did not find that, he said, "Uh-huh, he did not know what to look for!" So now, he just about gave me his name. Schaeffer? His name is Schaeffer, he said.

"Okay, Schaeffer, what can we do so that we clean the whole thing so that the entrance is pleasant, so that people want to have that place and business is excellent?"

He got out of the building, stood in front of that magnetic field and grabbed it, and pulled the balance of that disc from under that building. I thought it was only half of it a disc, but it was a complete disc. Half was pushed under the building, at the door, so he is pulling it out.

And I explained to Schaeffer: "Do you know that in the vibration you are in—the space you are in—you can use that like a flying saucer, to go to the Light?"
He said, "Come on!"

I said, "Yup, got to do it!"

All the boxes are now on that flying saucer. Oh, yes! But now I would like him to tie it very well, to make sure the boxes are staying on the flying saucer, and that he has something to hold on to too.

He finds that I am funny now. So, to be able to put the ropes and everything, he is putting it even further, even further.

And then before he leaves, though, I would like him to give his blessings to the building, so that people that will do business there will do extremely well, that they will want to, and they will do well. And while he is at it, make sure that the other side is doing well, keeps doing well, even better than now.

(Long pause)

He grabbed the balance of the bottle there, and he is squeezing the thing and spraying both the left and right sides of the building.
He said, "We are going to give it a cleaning job!"

You should see, he is squeezing that thing, let me tell you.

"Okay," he said, "and while we are at it, we must also spray above it, so whatever it is will fall on the roof."

As that disc is gone from under the building and is loaded high, I am curling the sides to make it like a pie plate to make sure everything stays on it. And I am going along for the flight to the Light, and when we are in front of the Light, I stop that flying saucer, so to speak, because I want to get off.

He too enjoyed the flight. He is quite a character, that guy has quite a sense of humor, let me tell you! So, bye! He went through the Light on his flying saucer loaded with all his personal belongings, and I am back in front of that building now.

I am doing something where that disc was. I am going to do something that incorporates the site doing well too. And it is a carpet, with "Welcome" on it.

(Pause)

And now I can easily go inside the building, and something is pulling me back outside, in front of that door. And I am putting a climbing rose bush, in my mind, that makes, like, an archway, above that door. And I am impressing it on the building now. And although people won't see it, there will be something there. And a "Welcome" carpet there in front of the door.
Although empty the vacant bay was inviting and peaceful now. Remembering Schaeffer impersonating the Four of Pentacles, I decided to impress Pentacles on the floor in the middle of that building. It is the energy of money—money, in the sense of good business. Excellent, excellent, excellent business. And that is it.

That guy was something else. That was most unusual. Schaeffer. Quite a sense of humor too. He used to make a lot of money in that building.

End of the session.

The owner of the strip mall contacted me a few weeks later to announce he had secured the vacant bay two weeks after the session, with a seven-year lease. Research confirmed that a gambling parlor was located right in the middle of the empty bay years ago.

The owner also reported that all the tenants in that strip mall were very happy, doing excellent business.

CHAPTER 6

Chapter - 6 -

Home At Last

Is living in the pure Energy Field many times called eternity, hell or heaven?

Do you wonder what happens next, when leaving the land where ghosts are roaming? What happens after going through the Light and entering what is commonly known as eternity? How is it? What does it look like?

The spirits who contacted me made me understand that with self-acceptance and inner peace, the time of reflection is paradise, heaven. However, once home in the Energy Field, the self-judgment becomes unbearable, pure hell, enticing the spirit to plan the next physical experience in an attempt to atone for what sits so heavily on the conscience. The last thought at the time of death is important. Self-acceptance and inner peace are truly the keys to paradise, heaven, nirvana, however one calls it.

About three months after his death, a man appeared to me at home on a bright afternoon. Well dressed, the man looked like a photograph of himself in his thirties. I could see only the outline of his face, an indication he had gone home, through the Light. Of all the people he had had to deal with, I had been the only one who had stood up to that tyrant. His ether body floating about 10 centimeters off the ground, he looked taller than usual.

That man hated me, and he must have gotten my telepathic question: *"What are you doing here, and what are you coming to see me for?"*

In a strong telepathic voice, he said, *"I am coming here to ask you for forgiveness for all the sorrow I caused you."*

The concept of time is part of our physical experience and is nonexistent once the physical body is shed.

A little more than twenty years later, the same man appeared to a highly psychic friend of mine. My friend knew immediately who he was, although she had never met him or even seen a picture of him, and he was seldom mentioned in a conversation or a reading. As the strong psychic conversation unfolded, he explained his reason to appear to her, defending his case in the hope she could get me to forgive him.

Personally, I truly do not care.

My feeling for that man had turned to indifference years before his death. He is still, in fact, attempting to convince himself he had done a lot of good. Obviously, no matter mine – or anyone else's response, he is the one who cannot forgive himself.

The story of Bernard

The following surrogate demonstration and training session was filmed during Hypnosis 601, Hypnotherapy and the Paranormal, at our campus in Hungary. The request for this surrogate session was to contact Bernard, who had died two years earlier. Elena, his widow, felt guilty at not having requested more medical intervention in the hope of saving his life. She also wanted to know what Bernard wanted to tell her as he died. Please note that she was in the classroom when the surrogate session was performed.

The first thing was to build a thick energy wall to stop any thoughts going on in the classroom, keeping maximum integrity for the session. After taking precautions, the following transpired.

Anny: *Bernard is there, he is there. Okay. I do not know what it is, but he has a pain here* (pointing to left side of upper chest, under left arm). *I do not know if I mirror him or what it is. It is pain here and also there is something like a block here* (upper throat, sides of neck), *and whatever it is, it is hurting here* (right side of jaw) *that part of the … here. It is almost like it is hurting his teeth on this side* (right).

He is not used to expressing his feelings, so he is doing everything to not cry. Everything to not cry. And I can feel my eyes welling up, but he will not show it, he will not show it.

I can see him staring at Elena. And he wants to cry, he wants to cry. He will not show it. So, I am going to ask him what is it that you want to say? What is it that you want to say? … He is frowning, I can feel the frowning, you know, I can feel the frowning …

And I can feel there is also a pain here (stroking right side of neck to jaw line) *that is coming up, so whatever it is, it is uncomfortable … Also, there is like … I am going to say what comes, okay? … It is like whatever comes, I do not know … He is given some medication that makes him feel very weak.*

I can feel my arms wanting to drop. And the head is turning. Whatever they put there, I do not know what it is, but it is really affecting the neck. So even … it is almost like he has … And he feels very, very, very, very, weak. Because my arms feel like (dropping arms). *Mm hmm … And he is looking at Elena … All that he does is looking at her. So, I would like to know, okay what is his name again? … I cannot remember his name …*

Facilitator: *Bernard.*

Anny: *"Bernard? Okay. I want you to tell me what is it that you feel that way?"*

And he is starting to get younger now, younger, ... It has something to do with the lifestyle, when he was younger. ... It is almost like there is a guilt feeling that sits here (stomach) *and huh ... is it not interesting? And whatever it is, it is really hard to swallow. ... Well, it is in a figurative way, of course. There is something ... there is a quiet regret or guilt feeling.*

Anny: *"What is it, Bernard, what is it? Come on. What is it? Just tell me. Make me understand what is it that you regret?" ...*
Bernard was not used to expressing his feelings, and many encouragements of doing so had to be done during the entire session, asking him to explain more and more.

It is a guilt feeling, not regret, a guilt feeling, about something. And he knows, he says, as he was dying, he knows that is where the whole thing started. All what I see, that is the only thing he shows me, is a table in front of a window, and I can see the city from the window. That is all that he would show me ...

But there is something there that makes him feel very guilty. And what I find interesting is that that table is just a bare wooden table. That is all that he will show me ... And then something about something he did. And then he looks at Elena again ... And he feels very weak, I am telling you, he feels ... I have no idea ... it smells like alcohol. Tastes like it too ...

He is making me aware that, if he could, he would have completely dismissed the first part of his life, if he could start his life at the middle of it, so to speak ... And he is looking at Elena, let me tell you. ... It is almost like his life is cut in two, the first part that he wished he never lived ...

He wishes he could have said, just before his last breath, that he loves her. And he is crying, I am telling you, he is crying inside. That is all that he wished he could have done, just before his last breath. That was his wish. He could not do it ...

Anny: *"So, anything else that you wish?"*

Hmm ... He wants Elena to know that his physical condition is from the first part of his life, whatever that means. I do not have a clue what it means. And it has something to do with the lifestyle. But he will not ... he is not willing to express it.
It is almost that he regrets so much the first part of his life, whatever he did or did not do, that he is cutting it off, so to speak. That even with me, he will not show me, it is almost like he wants to deny it, although he knows that is what brought the illness.

When asking him what could have been done for him to be healthy, he says completely erase the first part of his life, and he adds, "Nobody could do it."

Anny: *"And now that you are on the other side?"*

He says he cannot, even on the other side, because he thought by dying he could erase the first part of his life.
Bernard: *"But you know, it is still there."*

Anny: *"So what, according to where you are now, what will erase it?"*

Isn't that interesting? ... He said the only way to erase it is to live life again, starting right away, at the second part of the life he just left. With the same person. ... And he shows me Elena. And he feels like crying, crying, crying. Just crying, crying, crying.

Facilitator to Anny: *"Can I ask?"*

Anny: *"Any question?"*

Facilitator to Anny: *"Anny, ask him if anything in his body could heal himself? To be done differently or anything that you may be aware of that comes from him?"*

It was really the message he gave me. It is that he thought by dying it would remove the first part of his life. That is the reason he allowed himself to die. And he said it did not. It is still there ... major guilt feeling there. Whatever it was ... whatever it was ... But he feels so guilty about it that he is blocking it completely, because that is what he tried to do.

He really tried to block it in such a way that even though he knows what is behind that block, he denied it; he did everything to start fresh, so to speak. Whatever it was. But he was going as far as a bare table in front of a window ...

He knew he was going to die, and he let himself die. It was almost like, "I cannot stand whatever is creating the guilt." You know what, it was very simple. He was not going to fight for his life. He was not, no, he was not, no matter what. Because he really wanted to get rid of the first part of his life.

And he is so secretive about it that he will not show me ... no, nothing. Only that table in front of a window, looking at a city or whatever it is, and the place where it is. It is a little higher than the city, almost like on the side of a hill. Yes, there is a big hill there, so here I am again, in front of that window.

Facilitator to Anny: "Is there any information or anything to Elena or to anybody to resolve? Is there anything that he wished to do?"

Anny: "Oh, he is saying to me, that he keeps sending messages to Elena about being together again."

Bernard: "Well, I am going to tell you something. I am the one who put that in her head." And he is smiling for the first time. "She thinks it is her idea, he says, but it was mine."

Anny: Hmm, hmm. Men, huh?
And you know what, to have said that, he feels, like, relieved. It is almost like he admitted a secret, so to speak.

Facilitator to Anny: "Is there anything else that could have been done for him?"

No, he did not want to. ... No, he did not want to, there was something there that was heavy on him, and he did not want to. Having admitted that he is the one that is putting that idea in Elena's head made him feel so much lighter, and he even started to laugh, as if to say, "Ha!" It made such a difference to have admitted.

Facilitator to Anny: *"Can you check that, is there anything that he learned from this life here, and maybe something that needs to be different, needs to be said?"*

Anny: *"Bernard, what have you learned? What have you learned?" ...*

He learned, hmm. ... It is interesting.

He is explaining something to me, and it is that in the beginning of his life he did things to please, let us say, the establishment, whatever that means. ... It seems like family. And he learned, he learned that whatever you do, it has to be your choice. His choice, it has to be his choice, not what other people expect from him. And he says, "especially about marriage" ... and the screen went blank again. I must say that, now he is ... you know to have confessed that, that he is the one to be putting that in Elena's head, that made him chuckle.

Facilitator to Anny: *"Is there anything important to check, maybe his physical body, why was it, what happened?"*

Anny: *All that I know is that, we are going back to the beginning of the session here, and it is like rods here* (pointing to either side of neck), *and he could not communicate, so to speak. And is that interesting, that that man was ... and you know, the fact that he felt so good admitting that he is the one that is putting that idea in Elena's head ... is indicating ... and the rods there, not being able to talk ... all wanted to say was how much he loved her before he died.*

What happened is this: the whole thing is about communication. You know, it is saying what he really wanted to say, and he really never allowed himself to say what he wanted to say. Especially in the first part of his life.

Okay, just a moment here, just a moment here. ... I am asking him something, it came from him, and the thing is that he wanted to say something and did not. ... The restriction came again.

He is doing something ... he is now ... and it is simply something in and out. Bernard showed me approaching and touching Elena (who was in the room).

He just approached her like, you could say, a medicine man, something like that. And he is doing something here; there is something here he is doing (pointing to stomach) *for her to be in good health.*

And then he left, he did that. ... And you know, he is ... he went through the Light. He did. ... Because although I could see him, I could not see his face. I could feel the tears, the restriction here, there is something here (neck and right jaw), *whatever it is, my! I could feel it. I did not see his face.*

And I can sense his smile, although he does not have a face. And you know what he says now?
"I said everything I wanted to say, let me go back."

Anny: *"Okay, just go."*

And the screen is blank again.

Wrapping up end of session.

Elena confirmed the partying and heavy drinking lifestyle before Bernard met her. The struggle with the establishment and his family was a fanatic religious one about love and marriage.

The window was the window in an apartment building. When I described the window wide open, not seeing anything closing the window, I learned it was the way all the windows are in some countries: the hinges are in such a way that when the window is completely open—outward—one sees only the window frame.

The terrible feelings in Bernard's neck and jaw were caused by something the nurses had put in his throat to enable him to breathe, pushing on his jaw and teeth, keeping his mouth open so he could not speak. At one point he even attempted to remove the contraption from his mouth to tell something to Elena. The nurses put it quickly back in place and tied his hands at the wrists to the sides of the bed so he could not attempt to remove the device.

This session was truly a healing session for everyone concerned, allowing for closure of this unfinished business.

Conclusion:

Not everything signals the presence of a ghost!

There is a difference between being possessed and cursed.

Although clearly seeing it while in an altered state of awareness, a person usually does not know what is going on – the feeling being the same.

A possession is psychic interference coming from a deceased person. We call them entities and people, having no idea of who they are – we call them ghosts.

A curse is a thought form that materialized itself and can be clearly seen when in an altered state of awareness.

A curse can be made by one individual when thoughts are directed with great and powerful anger to a person.

Usually, a curse involves a ritual to send a specific thought to the subject they target. The subject then knows something is wrong and does not know what it is.

The person targeted sometimes has the impression that there is a ghost at play. The feeling being the same although there is no ghost involved – only someone alive.

In a surrogate session, I clearly see who and what kind of ritual is performed. It is interesting to observe how rituals vary from continent to continent.

About a year ago, I had an interesting one directed to our property.

A lady was part of a group enjoying sending "bad vibes" to people they felt were going to interfere with their psychic and lucrative activities.

Checking carefully the energy of our property each time I was in a deep hypnotic trance – I knew something was wrong and could not figure out what is was.

One day, while in a deep hypnotic trance, I decided to look up in the sky.

And there it was: Very high in the sky, a large black cloud over our entire property.

I then commanded the large dark cloud to return the energy to the rightful owners, and make sure the group would lose its psychic ability to do destructive work.

What I witnessed then could be part of a movie from outer space:

The dark cloud moved to the next province, stopped over a town and started to direct lightning to what looked like a large cauldron.

Talk about fireworks!
Attempting to climb out of the about three-meter-deep cauldron – a lady tried to flee. Despite her best efforts to avoid the dark cloud energy she created – the lightning hit her back into the cauldron.

And the energy of our property was peaceful again.

The road to what we call eternity, heaven

The road to what we call heaven is in two stages. We first enter where ghosts are roaming, and then we move on to the Universal Energy Field.

In the first stage, an earthbound spirit living where ghosts are roaming behaves the same way as when they were in physical form, with a difference: they do not have a physical body, and the majority of people do not see or hear them.

When they show themselves, they appear at the age of death, the way they physically looked before death, including what they were wearing. Some of the most profound information the earthbound spirits have taught me is that as disincarnate entities, ghosts exist and have no life.

Ghosts are disincarnating spirits very stuck in what they thought as they died. They are usually lost, having forgotten to go through the Light, so they are in thrall to what they were thinking as they left their body.

Being scared to leave this physical world is usually the reason they fight so much for what they think is their life, not acknowledging they exist in limbo between the physical world and the spirit world. Their bodies are of ether, of lesser density than in the physical plane. They can move through people, doors, buildings, mountains, anything that exists physically and bump into one another, since they are of the same density (or vibration). However, they cannot see through anything that is physical or material.

Staying earthbound is very much an individual experience, and sometimes a personal desire. It could be that someone is grieving for them, not wanting to let them go, as in Jodi's case. It could be jealously and possessiveness, making sure the surviving spouse will not find another (and better) companion. There are many more reasons, which is why I included many stories about spirits living where ghosts are roaming.

The important difference between being earthbound and being in the Light, heaven, eternity, whatever you call it is that an earthbound spirit cannot reincarnate. To reincarnate requires first returning into the Universal Energy Field, eternity, heaven.

In the second stage, once through the light, what sits heavily on one's conscience makes the sojourn in the ether hell, thus the decision to have another run at a physical life to atone and dissolve the feeling.
When totally at peace with all of our past experiences, then our sojourn in the ether is truly heaven, paradise. Once having gone *home* through the Light, when a spirit shows itself, they have the physical appearance of how they were in their mid-thirties—unless they died younger—with only the outline of their face showing. so the person they appear to knows who they are as well as what life they wish to heal.

Understanding the spirit world makes us also understand who we are. We are multidimensional beings, spirits that have chosen to experience this physical world. We are pure Energy. Everything is Energy—one could call it vibration—and Energy is everything. Energy is the life force that makes everything collective, the reason we can access someone else's information by accessing the universal consciousness, also known as the Akashic Records.

Because of this collectiveness, it is also true that each time we heal a part of ourselves, we help heal the world. The physical world is the densest of all. When on this physical plane, we bump into one another, collide, and must respect all the barriers in front of us—walls, doors, etc. When in the spirit world, we are at a lighter level of density and can move through people. We are spirits having a physical experience, and with proper training we can access both worlds. Truly, being a human is an incredible adventure.

Regardless of religion or the lack of it, regardless of gender, age, or ethnic background, my clients have taught me that at death, we all see *the Light*, the portal to go to *our house*. There are portals throughout the universe, wherever we are at time of death or when deciding to go through the Light after spending some time where ghosts are roaming.

By helping clients accessing past lives, connecting with disincarnated entities, ghosts, as well as Spirits having gone home, through the portal of another dimension, I learned that hell or heaven is not a place. It is a state of being.

We are the only one to judge us when entering the other side of life, and once there, our spirit does not float in a long white robe, playing the harp, a halo of sainthood over our head. We take our conscience with us. We are the ones who are making this physical experience hell or heaven, the same as when we are on the other side, the nonphysical side of life. We are the ones who are judging ourselves, and how we feel about ourselves makes life on the other side either hell or heaven. When it is hell, it compels us to come back to atone, get rid of what torments us. Yes, our last thoughts are that important.

As I was growing up, heaven was up, and hell was below, and that never made sense to me. I was living three degrees below the equator. I was living *below* and it was sure nice living there!

Listening to my clients, having done this type of work for so many years, I also started to understand why God, however or whoever we perceive God to be, is omnipotent, alive and everywhere. I also have an idea of where *our house* is. I do not know any details of it, though. Life can be quite a mystery at times. Yes, there is still so much to learn.

Afterword

There are many ways to understand what we call the afterlife, depending on our philosophy of life.

Listening with great attention to what the spirits explained with candor confirms that we are eternal beings. Our soul lives forever and our physical being is just a shell that we choose to take on for whatever we decide to experience and then voluntarily discard to return to eternity, that place in the Universal Energy.

Spirits living where ghosts are roaming have the ability to attach themselves to anything, infusing their energy to accomplish whatever they set themselves up to do. Spirits can reincarnate only once they are in the Universal Energy Field, heaven, or whatever you call that place in eternity.

The reason a soul would want to experience life on this physical plane is individual. Everything is planned in advance to fulfill the "what for." How we go about it will make it a success or a failure.

I do understand that not everyone will comprehend or believe what was explained here. It was not the purpose either. What I hope it did is help you to have a good look at yourself without judgment, realizing who you really are.

Realizing we are eternal beings, it is important to be at peace with what we decide to challenge ourselves with and set out to resolve. The outcome could then be gratifying beyond belief.

Anny Slegten

Hypnotherapy, A Healing Modality

There are many healing resources. The choice will be governed by how fast one wants to advance in life.

As a hypnotherapist, I understand that the reason a person seeks help is usually a symptom of something different, many times seemingly out of context and only making sense to the client.

Hypnosis can be done over the telephone. However, for hypnotherapy, using hypnosis to facilitate therapy, personal contact is necessary. There are many nonverbal communications like a tremor in the voice, facial expressions, shifting as we talk, and even physical odor that has nothing to do with hygiene that allow the hypnotherapist to understand and effectively help the client.

From the results clients are reporting, a surrogate hypnotherapy session is by far the most potent. During a surrogate session, we are in fact reading the client in a way that can be experienced only in that modality.

In my experience, the purpose of the session is an investigation or healing session for everyone concerned. Reading a client with my five senses, I then switch and become the hypnotherapist.

When doing the deep trance hypnotherapy, reading in front of the person who requested the healing, much energy is required to constantly block the client's thoughts, to get a pure answer.

The best and most effective results are by far doing the session while the person is absent, not knowing the day and time their session will be performed. Whether a one-on-one hypnotherapy session or a hypnotherapy session at a distance by surrogate, the number of sessions depends on the client.

In my experience, any work involving what one would call a mental illness may require up to four surrogate hypnotherapy sessions, occasionally more, to clear the emotional cause leading to the physical symptoms. During a surrogate hypnotherapy reading session, all information comes from a nonphysical source.

I am not a physician, and I do not claim to heal any medical condition. Over the years, I learned that the way a person was told of their physical condition can be the catalyst of the outcome. I only do whatever is possible for my clients to shift into the results they are seeking.

Yes, as potent as a one on one hypnotherapy session or surrogate hypnotherapy reading session is, only the client can make the necessary shift. No one, not even me, can do it for them.

Complete information on this subject can be found by visiting

http://www.success-and-more.com/services.html

Having never experienced being in a hypnotic trance that they are aware of, some people have an interesting idea of what being hypnotized is.

As explained before, no matter what, the person in a hypnotic trance is always in total control. Yes, a person can lie through their teeth if they choose to do so.

Not feeling safe by having a one on one hypnotherapy session or a virtual hypnotherapy session, a person asked if meditation would work too.

There is a difference between hypnosis and meditation, which is noticed by brainwaves during hypnosis and meditation by HZ, or cycles/second.

Hypnosis shows a much slower cycle than meditation.

Voltage between head and other parts of the body become more negative during physical activity, decline in sleep, and reverse to positive under general anesthesia.

It is a change in voltage.

Information from:
The Body Electric

By Roberts O. Becker, MD and Gary Selden

To my understanding, meditation connects with the brain and hypnosis allows us to connect with the mind.

Do you wonder how come I have a picture of my recliner printed on some pages?

After all, it is only a recliner, or so you may think!

At the end of a highly emotional and delightful hypnotherapy session involving his relationship with his father, a man in his mid-twenties got up and, pointing to my recliner said, "This is a magic chair!"

Since then, the picture of my recliner has been my trademark.
I recently had to put it in retirement, worn out after thirty-one years of constant use. I had to hold the back of the recliner for fear of the chair flipping back to the floor when put in the recliner position.

It is with relief that I observe the new recliner has taken over the magic side of the hypnotherapy sessions.

Online Store, Contact, And More...

You may contact Anny by visiting any of her websites and scroll down the home page to the contact information.

https://www.annyslegten.com
Anny's private website and online store.

This is the best place to keep up to date with Anny – including seeing all her latest books and how to order them on Amazon.

https://www.success-and-more.com
To find the description of the many services offered, and more.

https://www.htialberta.com
The Hypnotism Training Institute of Alberta including descriptions of hypnosis and hypnotherapy courses given.

https://www.reiki-canada.com
About the Reiki Training Centre of Canada.

https://www.slegtenianhypnosis.com
Although open to anyone interested in this fascinating hypnosis modality, this website information is for graduates of the Hypnotism Training Institute of Alberta.

Other Books By Anny

Other books published by Anny Slegten can be found at:

https://www.annyslegten.com/books

as well as ordering on Amazon when deciding to buy a book.

Glossary / Description

Akashic Records

Everything is Energy and Energy is everything, the reason we can access any information when tuning in to the right wavelength, frequency.

All the information available about *Akashic* explains that the name comes from *akasha*, a 5,000-year-old Sanskrit word that means "sky", "air", "open space".

Since Energy is everything and everything is Energy, the Universal Energy that fills the akasha (sky, air, open spaces) is impregnated with everything that ever happened and existed and is referred to as the Akashic Records, the information stored in the sky.

From my experience, to access the information stored into the Universal Energy Field, all that is required is to go in a deep hypnotic trance, consciously entering the mind, our non-physical part that is part of the Universal Energy Field, and tune into the right vibration frequency.

Alter

An earthbound entity who attached itself to a living person.

Belgian Congo

Straddling the equator, an African colony of Belgium until its independence in June 1959. It then for a time was called Zaire and is now La République Démocratique du Congo.

Belgium

A small, bilingual country in Europe nestled between The Netherlands, Germany, Luxembourg, France and the North Sea. The capital of Belgium is Brussels, home of *Manneken Pis*.

Depossession

Better understood as exorcism, releasing the alter from the host, freeing the host, and sending the alter, the earthbound entity, the ghost to complete their journey and enter into the Universal Energy Field.

Earthbound entity

Once having discarded the physical part of self, the spirit or the soul becomes earthbound when not moving forward into the Universal Energy Field, the second part of afterlife.

Energy

In this context, Energy refers to the Universal Energy; one could call it the God Head. It is that intangible something that exists, very different from the energy sector we humans are attempting to create, not knowing how to tap into the Energy that exists in the universe. It is the Energy of the Divine, whoever or whatever one perceives the Divine to be.

Entity

Once dead and not moved forward, an entity is a ghost living where ghosts are roaming, who makes itself a life by attaching itself to an object, a place or a person, influencing who or what they attached themselves to. In a way, it is a person living without a body and becomes a parasite to make itself alive.

Everett, Hugh III

Hugh Everett III (November 11, 1930–July 19, 1982) was an American physicist who first proposed the many-worlds interpretation (MWI) of quantum physics, which he termed his *relative state* formulation

Ghost

To my understanding, a ghost is the spirit of a dead person living where ghosts are roaming, confused and stuck, with no particular idea or focus, not knowing they exist and have no life.

Hypnosis, Hypnotherapy

Hypnosis is a technique to connect with the mind and manipulate the brain. Hypnotherapy requires more training. It is using hypnosis, the tool, to do therapy. For example, hypnosis is used during childbirth to relax and experience a comfortable and natural birthing experience. Hypnotherapy is used to go to the cause of any concern about having children, pregnancy, and anything related to the birth of a family.

Hypnotism Training Institute of Alberta

The hypnosis school run by Anny Slegten. In Canada, a school denotes a teaching business, not a building where you go to school.

Host

The person who is possessed by an earthbound entity.

Kalina

An area in Léopoldville.

Léopoldville, Kinshasa

Léopoldville, capital of Belgian Congo. At the country's independence, the name reverted to the familiar name of Kinshasa.

Les Dames du Sacré Cœur

A religious order dedicated to the veneration of the Heart of Jesus, the Christ. Its inception dates from around 1800 by a Jesuit and Madeleine-Sophie Barat. The Belgian Mother House was in Jette near Brussels, Belgium.

Neuro Linguistic Programming (NLP)

Dr. Milton Erickson (1901–80) an American psychiatrist that had an enormous influence on the practice of both clinical hypnosis and the exquisite use of verbal and nonverbal communication. Having observed filmed therapeutic sessions of Erickson, and wanting to create the same apparent outcome, Richard Bandler and John Grinder developed a unique approach of communication to influence the brain; and Neuro Linguistic Programming (NLP) was created.

Penfield, Wilder

Wilder Penfield (1891–1976) was the founder of the Montreal Neurological Institute, and one of the greatest neuroscientists who ever lived. In his many research experiments, Penfield reported that there is no place in the cerebral cortex where electrical stimulation will cause a patient to believe, decide or will. These are not functions of brain, but of the "I," or soul.

The brain is physical. The mind is nonphysical and is connected to the soul.

Pentacle

Pentacles are symbols in Tarot cards, which are used for divination. To me, they represent abundance and good fortune in one form or another, the result of labor. The Four of Pentacles I refer to in *Stories from the Other Side* is from the Albano-Waite deck.

Portal

The Light directing a soul into the Universal Energy Field that shows itself at time of physical death.

Reiki

Originating in Japan and developed by Mikao Usui, Reiki is one of the best-organized ways to teach and learn energy work in one weekend. It is a form of laying on of hands with a focus on healing and relaxation.

Spirit

Spirit refers to the Energy, the soul, the essence of being, part of the Universal Energy Field, eternity, heaven, paradise—whatever you call that place.

Travois

Two trailing poles attached to a horse with a net or a platform secured at the end and used to carry loads.

Where ghosts are roaming

A name I give for purgatory, limbo, a grey area. It denotes the space a soul enters when discarding the physical body and before entering the Universal Energy Field. It is a place and condition between physical life and eternity

About Anny - The Author

Belgian-born, Anny Slegten lived in Belgian Congo until coming to Canada.

A full-time clinical hypnotherapist since 1984, Anny has initiated many therapeutic techniques she then teaches in Canada and around the world.

Today, she has built her personal interest and natural affinity for helping people into a thriving counselling practice and a well-respected training institute. Anny operates her busy counselling and teaching facility and has expanded from providing individual sessions to teaching, including introductions and certification to aspiring students. Many of her students are international, and she has recently returned from a trip to Hungary, where she reconnects every second year with some of her fellow hypnotherapist practitioners and teaches classes.

Founder and Director of the Canadian Institute of Hypnosis, Kinesiology and Complementary Therapies, Anny is presently Director of the Hypnotism Training Institute of Alberta, where she formulates hypnosis and hypnotherapy courses. Anny, for instance, developed a program for the Hypno-Baby Birthing Facilitator Certification in collaboration with an obstetrician and a nurse.

Anny holds many certifications in hypnosis and hypnotherapy. Anny has also studied a wide variety of disciplines to complement and augment her skills as a hypnotherapist under the tutelage of global leaders

Fascinated with how the mind works, she now adds writing articles and books to her busy schedule, sharing what her clients have taught her.

Anny Slegten's students arrive at her office from all walks of life, levels of education from professionals to young adults with no formal post-secondary education and are from across a broad spectrum of society, racial origin, religious belief, and life experience.

Their reasons for being there are as diverse as their backgrounds: some are exploring career options, some have had healing by Anny when all else has failed in attempts to own themselves, and some purely due to Anny's reputation. They are truly a gathering of a "mini United Nations ".but when they leave they all have so very much in common and have shared deeply of themselves under Anny's superb tutelage.

What becomes increasingly obvious as students progress on their journey is that Anny is indeed unique as a person and a professional. Her stringent personal, professional and spiritual ethics shine through in all she does and teaches and her generosity in sharing any newly acquired knowledge in annual updates for her graduates is well known and appreciated by all. Anny is truly gifted in seeing all people and entities as worthy of her respect and she imparts this to her students.

In Anny's very interactive classroom all soon come to recognize that while there are very effective and successful hypnotherapists internationally, Anny Slegten's unique qualities and methods ensure that all have the opportunity to developed the skills to successfully improve their lives and if they chose to do so, to enter a full practice on leaving HTI of A with the experience and knowledge to confidentially address any issue or entity that should arrive in their personal lives and practices.

As many of Anny's students have successfully progressed in their private lives and careers, they have strongly urged Anny to brand her way of teaching and practicing hypnotherapy as Slegtenian Hypnosis.

To meet Anny, visit www.success-and-more.com; click on Anny Slegten.com and enjoy the visit.

Stories From The Other Side

www.ingramcontent.com/pod-product-compliance
Lightning Source LLC
LaVergne TN
LVHW011911080426
835508LV00007BA/476